SO-BET-609

ON THE LAST FRONTIER

On The Last Frontier

A History of
Upton County, Texas

BY

N. ETHIE EAGLETON

TEXAS WESTERN PRESS

THE UNIVERSITY OF TEXAS AT EL PASO

1971

Edited by

S. D. MYRES

Library of Congress Catalog Card No. 70-139679

ISBN 0-87404-027-2

This volume is dedicated as a permanent reminder of their contribution to Upton County history

- To Chapter 76, McCamey Junior Historians, whose interest in their county's history has kept alive a desire to continue search and research.

- To Mrs. Charles C. Green, Sr., whose keen appreciation and unstinted effort aided in the collection of records, data, and materials in the preparation of this work.

FOREWORD

For the past thirty years, I have assembled data for a history of Upton County. Many sources have been investigated. Many stories have been left untold, and many others might have been told better by someone else.

This work is a pioneer volume. I am indebted first of all to the Chapter 76, McCamey Junior Historians for their papers filled with information on early happenings in Upton County. Then to the County Clerks, Miss Leta Powell of Crockett County, Mrs. Nancy K. Daugherty of Upton County, to the Deed Records of Buchel County, to Mrs. M. L. (Edith) Hopson, Manager of Trans-Pecos Abstract Company of Alpine, and to Mrs. Arthur (Roberta) Caldwell of Reagan County, I am indebted for access to the public records which confirmed the stories told by members of Chapter 76 and their parents.

Individuals who have lent their talents and offices are Mrs. Joe (Mary Lee) Conger of the McCamey High School Library; Elmer Kelton, Editor *Sheep and Goat Raiser*, San Angelo, Texas; Gene Kinney, the Robert Massie Funeral Chapel, San Angelo; Mrs. Frank (Annejo) Weeden, Marathon, Texas; Mrs. Norman (Ernestine Halff) Freeman, Dallas, Texas; George W. Ramer, McCamey, Texas; B. B. Inghram, a Crockett County rancher; Henry M. Hart, Vice-Chairman Executive Committee of Bank of Commerce, San Antonio, Texas; Jim Langdon, Chairman Railroad Commission, Texas; Cecil Gill, Humble Oil and Refining Company; John E. Reid of the Shell Oil Company; Mrs. George B. McCamey; Mrs. Olin Smith; Mrs. Lelyle (Harris) Russell; Mrs. J. Linton (Ann) Clark of Rankin, Texas; and Mrs. William Wolf. Howard Wolf, as a law student in the University of Texas, ferreted from the collection of rare books in the Law Library *The Journals of the Texas Legislative Manuals* 1879-1880; and 1882-1883. Diantha Dawkins researched in the Barker History Center. Mrs. Ada Phillips of Midland, Texas, rendered invaluable assistance with research in the Midland Museum. The Upton County Tax Assessor-Collector's Office and the office of the County Agent, W. M. (Dub) Day, Jr., also lent their time and efforts.

I would like to extend my deep appreciation to the Chairmen of the County Survey Committees, Mrs. John (Nancy Rankin) McKinney of Midland County; Mrs. Sue Navarro of Reeves County; Mr. Walter Freytag of Fayette County; and to Mrs. Ben E. Pickett of Liberty County; and to the Upton County Historical Committee, Mrs. Zack Monroe, Mrs. Opal Nix, Mrs. Jack Smith and Miss Maggie Taylor.

Archivists who have gone beyond the call of duty include Mrs. Marie Berry, San Antonio Library; Mrs. B. Brandt, Texas State Library; Miss Patricia Chadwell, Fort Worth Library; Dr. James Day, Texas State Archives; Mrs. Embry, Tennessee State Library and Archives, Nashville; Mrs. Ben Grissard, Franklin County Library, Winchester, Tennessee; Dr. Chester Keilman, University of Texas; Mrs. Carmen Perry, D.R.T., Library at the Alamo, San Antonio; Richard Santos, Bexar County Archivist, San Antonio; India W. Thomas, Confederate Memorial Library, Richmond, Virginia.

This volume would not have been possible without the help of Edith Windham, Patricia Wrinkle and Billie Sue Glass, who has been a ready and willing typist.

Lastly, I tender my appreciation to the Upton County Commissioners' Court and to County Judge Allen Moore, who have supported my efforts and who have seen fit to accept this volume as worthy of their sponsorship.

N. ETHIE EAGLETON

McCamey, Texas
September 1, 1971

CONTENTS

ON THE LAST FRONTIER

I

THE LAY OF THE LAND

UPTON COUNTY WAS NAMED FOR TWO BROTHERS, John Cunningham and William Felton Upton. It was one of six created out of western Tom Green County in 1887. The following act of the Legislature is basic:

New Counties created out of Tom Green County: 20th Legislature, Ch. 12 — H. B., No. 113 — An Act to divide the western portion of Tom Green County into six new counties.

SECTION I. Be it enacted by the Legislature of the State of Texas: That the following new counties shall be created out of the western portion of Tom Green County, and the boundaries thereof shall be as follows:

(d) The County of Upton: commencing at the southeast corner of Midland County, thirty-one 8/10 miles to the northeast corner of Crane County; thence, south thirty-six miles to the north boundary line of Crockett County thence thirty-one 8/10 miles; thence, north thirty-six miles to the place of the beginning. . . .

SECTION II. (d) The County of Upton is named in honor of Colonel John Upton, who was killed at the head of his regiment, gloriously leading the same in the charge of the Second Battle of Manassas, and his distinguished brother, the Hon. William F. Upton, lately deceased.

The foregoing act originated in the House, and was passed by a vote of 78 yeas, 1 nay; it passed in the Senate by 24 yeas, no nays. It was approved, February 26, 1887.

This semi-arid land lay open for range purposes. Imagine a diagonal line from the northwest corner of the boundary of Upton County to the southeast corner of the county. This line will divide the county approximately in the northeastern part into a rolling prairie with numerous small intermittent lakes, while the southwestern part has mesas reaching from 2700 feet to 3125 feet. Castle Mountain rises to 3125 feet and drops abruptly to 2900 feet to form a gap with King Mountain to the south, reaching an elevation of 3100 feet. King Mountain, like a huge dinosaur, sprawls eleven and a half miles to the south with a width of eight and a half miles. Some five miles to the south the Bobcat Hills lie, and to the east of King Mountain there are Square Top Mesa, Table Top Mesa and Rattlesnake Butte.[1]

Many unnamed draws run from these elevations. Centralia Draw heads up near the central part of the county and is a tributary to the

[1]

Middle Concho, which in turn is a tributary of the Colorado River. To the south heading up at Flat Rock is Rankin Creek, dry most of the time, wandering around until it joins the Five Mile Draw, known in the Open Range days as the J. M. Draw. Likewise, from the north Wild China Creek, and from the west many draws, drain into the J. M., which eventually makes its way into the Pecos River at Pontoon Crossing.

The weathering of this area through ages past has produced rock shelters in the broken areas. Plant life emerges in Upton County when there is enough moisture. It is appropriate to list at this point grasses which are our basic heritage and a neglected resource:

Alkali sacaton	*Sporobolus airoides*
Bermuda grass	*Cynodon dactylon*
Blue grama	*Bouteloua eriopoda*
Buffalo grass	*Buchloe dactyloides*
Burro grass	*Scleropogon brevifolius*
Bush muhly	*Muhlenbergia porteri*
Curly mesquite	*Hilaria belangeri*
Hairy grama	*Bouteloua hirsuta*
Hooded windmill grass	*Chloris cucullata*
Italian ryegrass	*Lolium multiflorum*
Red grama	*Bouteloua trifida*
Sand dropseed	*Sporobolus cryptandrus*
Sand lovegrass	*Eragrostis trichodes*
Seashore saltgrass	*Distichlis spicata*
Texas grama	*Bouteloua rigidiseta*
Tobosa grass	*Hilaria mutica*
Vine mesquite	*Panicum obtusum*
Wright threeawn	*Aristida wrightii*[2]

Certain shrubs and trees may be found also in Upton County:

Prairie Guajello	*Acacia augustissema*
Long Flowered Catclaw	*Acacia greggii*
Round Flowered Catclaw	*Acacia rolmerlana scheebe*
Tree Catclaw	*Acacia wrightii*
Mountain Redbud	*Cercis occidentalis*
Mesquite	*Prosopis chilensis*
Cresote Bush	*Larrea tridentata*
Cresote Bush-Guayacan	*Porlieria agust infolia*
Allthorn	*Koeberlinia spinosa*
Wild China	*Sapindus drummondii*
Ocotillo	*Fouquieria splendens*
Desert Willow	*Chilopsis linearis*
Blue Sage	*Salvia agurea*
Agave	*Lechuguilla*

Certain yuccas are native to Upton County: the Yucca glauca and the Yucca Macrocarpa, or the western dagger.[3]

William Felton Upton for whom Upton County, Texas was named, served as a representative from the 70th District to the 11th, 16th, 17th, 18th and 19th Legislatures of Texas.

R. A. Caldwell and N. Ethie Eagleton stand beside a large aerial map of Upton County made by Cecil Gill of Humble Oil and Refining Company.

Main Street of Rankin, Texas in 1930.

Upland School students, before 1910.

McCamey School band, 1934. Drummers were William Fulton and Junior Wells. First row, Kenneth Rogers, James Talley, Billy Edwards, Bob Stallworth, Donald McDougal, Mary McNamara, Faye Patton, Jerry Bass, Bobby Gassett, and Gwenn Pounds. Second row, Mr. Collins, Lester Jones, William Bass, Tommy Fuller, Perry Stokes, and Lee Burnham. Third row, Charles Ham, Deward Cook, Forest Parks, Darden McCollum, Leon Harris, and Charles Vail.

McCamey Junior Historians, Chapter 76. This group photo was made in 1942.

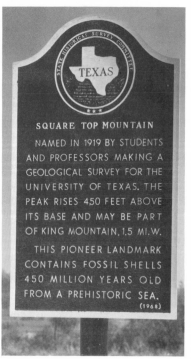

TEXAS

SQUARE TOP MOUNTAIN

NAMED IN 1919 BY STUDENTS
AND PROFESSORS MAKING A
GEOLOGICAL SURVEY FOR THE
UNIVERSITY OF TEXAS. THE
PEAK RISES 450 FEET ABOVE
ITS BASE AND MAY BE PART
OF KING MOUNTAIN, 1.5 MI. W.

THIS PIONEER LANDMARK
CONTAINS FOSSIL SHELLS
450 MILLION YEARS OLD
FROM A PREHISTORIC SEA.
(1968)

*Square Top Mountain Marker
on Highway 67.*

TEXAS

CASTLE GAP

Castle Gap Marker on Highway 67.

An abundance of cactus plants of numberless varieties were observed as Waterman Ormsby passed through Upton County in 1848.[4]

In retracing the Butterfield Overland Mail through Upton County in 1930, Mr. and Mrs. Roscoe Conkling indicate that "additional varieties of the cactus tribe and other desert flora make their appearance, warning of the proximity of arid or semi-arid zone." Referring to Castle Gap, they state:

Here on the protected eastern and southern castellated slopes of the mountains is one of the most beautiful natural cactus gardens along the route. The profusion of species characteristic of the Texas region is remarkable. The picture is enhanced at certain seasons of the year by myriads of flame-tipped ocotillo (Fouquieria splendens). Of the 202 species in the United States, 96 species, or nearly 48%, grow in Texas.[5]

Of the 96 varieties of cactus in Texas, 42 varieties may be found in Upton County.[6]

The annual precipitation of the area is from 10 to 15 inches. The winds are hot and dry in the summer. In the winter they come in from the Great Plains and the Chihuahua Desert and are often laden with sand and dust. They determine the plant cover of the area.[7]

The average precipitation[8] in McCamey from 1933 to 1952 was 14.12 inches. The lowest measurable rainfall was in 1933 when it fell to 7.67 inches and again in 1934 when it measured 7.69 inches. In 1940 the rainfall measured 17.55 inches, but in 1941 it measured 28.98 inches, causing the desert to be ablaze with wild flowers.

Imagine the excitement in 1941 when a new variety was brought to the classrooms by students from King Mountain and its draws, from the prairies and from the railroad dumps. The classes were divided into two groups; one group was to identify all purple and white flowers; the other was to identify the yellow and red flowers. The students spent their recesses and some class periods with all the Wild Flower books they could lay their hands on. Pairs sat together and identified seventy-nine different varieties of wild flowers, the seed from which blew into the county. The children planned a Wild Flower Show staged in the Elementary School Library on Mother's Day, 1941. Their teacher realized the great importance of this activity. She pressed all seventy-nine varieties and wrote their descriptions, being careful to make correct bibliographical notes. She registered for summer school at East Texas State Teachers College in 1942 for an Education Workshop. Among various requirements stipulated by the Registrar, the Heads of the Education, the Nature Study, the Botany and the Biology departments, there was one requirement made by each department — that blueprints of each of the seventy-nine varieties[9] be made. This was done and the prints were left with the school. The writer likewise made a duplicate

of the blueprints which were displayed at the McCamey Garden Club
and later given to the Mendoza Trail Museum, and still later filed in
the Upton County Archives.

From 1951 to 1960 the average annual precipitation was 13.23 inches.
The minimum amount of rainfall was 5.57 inches in 1953, and in 1954
it was 5.77 inches, thus reducing the amount of grass and other vegetation; however, in 1958 the measurement of moisture was 14.58 inches,
and in 1959 it was 19.40 inches. Then in 1960 the measurement in Mc-
Camey was 15.08 inches.[10]

Very little water reaches the draws and the streams. Drainage toward
the east flows into the Middle Concho River, and in the southwest it
goes toward the Pecos River to the south and west.

As an extra-curricular activity in high school sophomore Biology,
Lanny Menefee collected an exhibit of fossils from the flat-topped mesas
and buttes in Upton County, classified them and presented them to the
Mendoza Trail Museum in McCamey. In the collection there are two
Blastoridea, flower-like forms fixed to the bottom of the sea (Permian),
5 to 40 joints to the stem, forming a forest-like scene belonging to the
Upper Pre-Cambrian Group.[11] Menefee included eight specimens of
Gastropods in his collection of many different varieties.[12] One curious
specimen was a horn shell in a sword shape and form, estimated to be
270 million years old. Three specimens of Echinorides estimated at 120
million years were also included in the collection. Seven specimens
classified by Lanny Menefee belong to the Ordivician Period lasting
from 60 to 90 million years.[13] Most of these were found on Table Top,
Square Top and Flat Mesas and on Rattlesnake Butte in Upton County.

The rough, stony land in Upton County lying within the Edwards
Plateau results from erosion which exposed underlying limestone. After
the hard limestone was cut through, the erosion of the underlying softer
materials was rapid. This land is characterized by its rugged surface,
including small mesas having steep, rough slopes.[14]

The native vegetation varies somewhat with the texture of the soil.
Heavier soils support growth of chaparral, mesquite trees and cedar,
and the most common grasses are needle, tobosa, wire, grama and curly
mesquite. On the lighter textured soil, mesquite trees, yucca and cat-
claw grow, and the most common grasses are needle and buffalo.

The Reagan silty clay loam occurs in large bodies in Southern Upton
County. Reagan silty clay loam lies northwest of Rankin in the vicinity
of the McElroy Ranch Headquarters.

II

THE FORERUNNERS

IN THE SAND DUNES, in the deserts, and in the mesas of West Texas may be found a growing accumulation of relics and tools left by the Pecos people who, according to their own account, originated in the north and shifted southward to the head of the Pecos in the Sangre de Cristo Mountains.[15]

The Pecos River flows between the two areas of Central and West Texas, and the people of the Pecos adapted their artifacts to fit their needs. One such tool was the corner tang. In October of 1960 a bracero herding sheep on the McDonald Mesa, three miles south of the Pecos River in Pecos County, found a five-inch corner tang in a washout as he came down the mesa. A few days later, twelve-year-old Roy McDonald retraced the path of the bracero and at the same washout found a finely chiseled pendant. The lad left the location hurriedly when a drove of peccaries approached. He and his two brothers and three sisters often in the Fall of the year had a race with the racoons to get the persimmons that grow in the draws of the mesa. The mesa covers a wide area, and surveys indicate the flat top covers three sections of land.[16]

In the winter of 1960-61, the McCamey Junior Historians (Chapter 76), hiked to the top of McDonald Mesa, and from its top, they could see in the distance Blue Mountain in Upton County twenty miles away, along with King Mountain, Table Top, Square Top and Flat Top. Rock shelters in these sites harbored many campsites which can easily be identified from the air by the charred remains of the sotol pits. The findings here are typical of what may be discovered in the mesas along the Pecos. Here and along the trails leading from the Pecos River may be found a key to one of the oldest cultures on the North America continent.

Dr. J. E. Pearce of the University of Texas in 1938 wrote that the quality of the projectile points, the finely chipped knives and the snub-nosed scrapers were of a much finer quality than those found in other parts of Texas.[17]

In his translation of *The Expedition of Narváez, 1539*, Herbert Davenport pointed out that the Jumanos hunted deer and bison to the north and dressed the hides of deer, antelope and jack rabbits. Espejo in 1582 referred to the people along the Pecos as "Jumanos." Fray de Salas visited the Jumanos from 1598 to 1632, and they welcomed him and the missionaries with him. The Indians presented them with hides and pearls.[18]

On January 1, 1684, Domingues Mendoza, with a party of priests and soldiers, left La Junta (where the three forks of the Concho River join in Mexico to flow into the Rio Grande) in a northward direction to the Salado (Pecos River in Texas). On January 13 he sent out a party to examine the salt lakes up the river.[19] Upon the party's return, the expedition followed down the river approximately twenty-three miles, where he crossed over to the ranchería of the Jediondas, a tribe of the Jumano nation.[20]

Sabeata, a chief of the Jumanos, had gone with a delegation of two hundred Jumanos from the Conchos (Texas) and Pecos rivers to plead with Governor Cruzate at El Paso to send them soldiers to protect them from the Apaches. The Governor sent Dominguez Mendoza to look into their problem. When Mendoza's expedition reached a high rock hill, he proceeded to pitch his camp on the top of this hill, which he called Mount Honofre. Here he spent seven days where he held council with the chiefs of the Jumano nation. They plead with him to send soldiers and priests to protect them from the Apaches. Mendoza promised to consider their pleas. Then he proceeded to the Concho River (Texas).[21]

By 1777-1778 the Spanish proposed a campaign to exterminate the Apaches, but nothing came of this plan.[22]

Dr. Henry Connelly, a merchant in Chihuahua, Mexico, blazed a trail in 1839 across the Pecos at Old 'Dobe Crossing, then by way of Powell Gap to Wild China Pond in Upton County and on to Independence, Missouri, with a load of silver.[23]

The Chihuahua Trail was laid out from Chihuahua, Mexico, to Indianola, Texas, a distance of 1,150 miles. In blazing this trail, a small group of pioneers, including John W. Spencer and August Saltenberg, crossed at Horsehead Crossing, came through Castle Gap toward Wild China Pond down the Centralia Draw and on their way to Indianola. By 1869 trade had reached such substantial proportions that an auxiliary route by way of Sheffield near Fort Lancaster was used.[24]

When R. S. Neighbors, Chairman of the Texas-Mexican Boundary Commission, was guided in 1849 from Torey's Trading House through the Comanche lands by friendly Indians, he came up the Middle Concho westward on to Centralia Draw and on to Wild China Pond. Here at Wild China Pond on April 15 a norther blew up, bringing rain, sleet, snow and hail. The men were relieved when they reached Castle Gap. Dr. John (Rip) Ford rode ahead of the party. He was startled by a

Comanche Indian and his squaw. The Comanche threatened Ford just as Tall Tree, a guide, came to Ford's rescue. Tall Tree recognized the Comanche. They sat down for a powwow. When the Comanche learned that the surveyors were short on food, he killed and barbecued a fat mule and fed Neighbors and his party.

Major Neighbors, who was on his way to El Paso, passed several caravans. One caravan had forty-five wagons and another had forty. They were headed for California.[25]

On an expedition for the United States Army, John Russell Bartlett described his passage through this semi-desert county:

October 29, 1853. During the night we passed the spot marked on the map as Wild China Pond, which like the places before referred to, was destitute of water. Great mischief is caused by marking such places on maps, and had we not been told that it was doubtful whether water would be found there, we might have been unprepared with a supply, and suffered accordingly. On my return from California in 1852, I met several parties of emigrants from Arkansas and Eastern Texas, who had followed our trail from Fredericksburg to El Paso, and who were loud in their denunciation of those who had advised them to take this road, and more so of those who furnished them maps, which deceived them as to watering places. They expected to find water at localities designated on the map and took no precautions in case meeting with none. . . . At Flat Rock and Wild China Pond they were disappointed. They looked about the desert without success. One party was seventy-two hours without tasting water and came near perishing. Many of their mules and cattle died; and such as had strength remaining hastened on to the Pecos. There had been no water at either of the places designated during the spring or summer, nor was there any in October or November when we crossed it.[26]

Thus, it may be seen that by 1858 John Butterfield, in blazing out his trail from St. Louis to San Francisco to carry mail and passengers, would naturally follow the Middle Concho, Centralia Draw, Wild China Pond, Castle Gap, and on to Horsehead Crossing on the Pecos River.[27]

The Civil War interrupted the service of the Butterfield Overland Mail. However, activities over the trails did not cease. Three brothers, Juan, Cesario and Bernado Torres in the 1850's obtained a contract to supply travelers from Chihuahua with various and sundry necessities ranging from horses for remounts to whatever food could be obtained. They carried on their business in tents at Comanche Springs. When Camp Stockton was established in 1858, they obtained permits from the United States to supply certain necessities. It is said that their business yielded a satisfactory income, especially from 1865 to 1870. In the meantime, in May of 1875, these men obtained a charter from the State of Texas to construct irrigation ditches from the Pecos River.[28]

The Jumano Range, lying west of the Edwards Plateau and north through the Llano Estacado, prior to the Texas Revolution, lay within the Bexar Department, which included the south and west portion of the state. Within this Department a tract was granted to Beale and Grant for colonization.[29] This land was overrun by wild horses and cattle. It was a region of open range with much brush.[30]

Ben Ficklin, an experienced frontiersman, was awarded the contract in 1870 to carry the United States mail and passengers from Fort Smith, Arkansas, to San Antonio and thence to El Paso. His headquarters were at Fort Concho on the Colorado River.[31] An old map at the Barker History Center of The University of Texas locates two mail stations. One on the Pecos River had the name of Ficklin and was located at the Old 'Dobe Crossing. The other was a short distance from Horsehead Crossing.[32]

In the spring of 1866 three men, John Chisum, Charles Goodnight and Oliver Loving, struck out from Palo Pinto County for the Horsehead Crossing on the Pecos River following the Butterfield Trail with 7,000 Longhorns. No cattleman had ever attempted to cross this 100-mile arid semi-desert from the Llano Estacado through what is now Upton County to the Horsehead Crossing on the Pecos.[33] Goodnight and Loving moved their cattle on to Colorado. The route they followed was known as the Goodnight-Loving Trail.

In 1872 a wagon train from Mississippi arrived at Castle Gap. According to Enoch Smith, his grandfather, Tol Dawson (then a three-year-old boy with his parents) was in the group. Years later, Tol told Enoch the story of an Indian siege at the gap. Since the wagon train members knew that Indians were near, a guard was placed at both ends of the gap. The Indians laid siege for several days. As a result, the wagon train's supply of water became exhausted, and several unsuccessful attempts were made to reach the Pecos. The group finally succeeded, but only after several had died from thirst; these victims were buried at Castle Gap, where rocks identified the graves. The surviving pioneers went further west, but later several returned to take up land claims. Enoch states that his grandfather settled just west of the gap, and at the time of his death in 1921 he owned most of this land south to Horsehead Crossing.[34]

In the early 1880's drought drove many families westward to the Fort Davis country. One wagon train camping at Castle Gap consisted of Mr. and Mrs. R. P. Bean and their young children; Mr. and Mrs. John Means with two children; and Mr. and Mrs. George W. Evans with two children. This three-family caravan pitched camp in the Davis Mountains, July 28, 1884. Their diaries reveal that the women drove the wagons, and the three men rode herd on more than seven hundred cattle. Their diaries also reveal that they camped in Castle Gap for several days. These pioneers established a firm foundation for their homes, their schools and for their religion. They were among the founders of the famous Bloys Camp Meeting.[35]

After the buffalo slaughter, which rid the region of the Comanches and Apaches, J. Wright Mooar and his brother, John W. Mooar, saw an opportunity for the settlement of the open range.[36]

A cache of interesting material was found in a rock shelter on Indian Mesa in eastern Pecos County approximately twenty miles southwest of McCamey by Mr. and Mrs. M. W. Humphreys on August 1, 1954. This cache revealed numerous articles including pouches of deerskin, antelope skin, and bison hide sewed with ocotillo fibres, numerous paint bags, parts of the sleeve of a calico dress, and various other articles. Mr. Humphreys presented this cache to the Mendoza Trail Museum, August 15, 1954.[37]

When Dr. George W. Elliott in 1881 bought land lying on Wild China Pond, the China Pond Creek, the Centralia Draw and the Castle Gap Creek (all tributaries of the Pecos River, in what was then Tom Green County), he was preparing for a herd of one thousand stocker cattle. Dr. Elliott built a two-room house of rocks and stones in the region. Instead of hauling water from the head of the Middle Concho some thirty miles away, he drilled a well thirty feet deep, furnishing his needs.[38] Dr. Elliott sold his Upton County spread to James Kennedy in 1890 and moved to Midland.[39]

Mayer Halff and his brother of San Antonio leased in 1890 from R. M. Hall, Commissioner of the General Land Office, Sec 1-18, Blk 15, 640 acres at 3¢ per acre per annum.[40] Extensive ranching interests of these brothers in the 1890's ranged from Independence Creek in Crockett County up through Upton County to within a few miles of Midland.[41] They had bought fifty surveys of land one section deep along the Pecos River south of Fort Lancaster, moving their Circle Dot stock here.[42] This tract later became their horse range. In the 1890's they were moving their J. M. stock across the Pecos River by way of Pontoon Crossing into the open range of Upton and Midland counties, following the Five Mile Creek, known locally as the J. M. Draw, to Wild China Pond and northward to a few miles south of Midland. By December 24, 1898, Mayer Halff and Brother began to purchase land in Upton County previously owned by Dr. George Elliott. At the turn of the century[43] M. Halff and Brother began the dissolution of their partnership, and M. Halff's son, Henry, joined his father in the operation of his ranch land in Upton and Midland Counties. This new partnership moved their headquarters from Pontoon Crossing on the Pecos to the old rock house (Dr. Elliott's), which served as headquarters for Circle Dot, the J. M.

and Quien Sabe activities. After the organization of Upton County, the old rock house served as a mail station, a salt house, a bunkhouse for cowboys and a storeroom.

J. M. Johnson and his brother Tom from San Angelo came to the open range near Old 'Dobe Crossing and ranched there until 1901. Their cattle brands were "Box J" and "Four Apples." In these wide open spaces came other ranchers hunting for grass and water. When they found them, they took possession, provided no one else had prior rights. They used what land they needed.[44]

According to Will Noelke, Andy Young in 1891 moved his horses, branded Y, from Coleman County to 'Dobe Crossing. Here a better supply of grass was available during most of the year. Young left his horses in charge of a ranch hand by the name of Wash Forbes. For his headquarters Forbes took over the old 'Dobe house east of the Pecos. Noelke stated that when the first frosts killed the grass and weeds, Forbes moved the horses to the 7D horse trap down the Pecos River. Here in the winter a fresh range could always be found.[45]

The father of Dee Locklin, A. D. Locklin, and Dee's uncle, Walter Smith, herded sheep (some 3,600) between "S" and Pontoon Crossing in the 1890's. They camped "under the stars" and drifted their flocks toward the grass. Smith loaded salt from Lake Cordona on a sled, transferring it to a wagon for the sheep down the Pecos.[46] Uncle Will Smith, a man who weighed only ninety-four pounds, entranced the Junior Historians in the fall of 1951 with his accounts of early days on the range. A poignant feeling was experienced by his hearers, for Mr. Smith was blind when he talked to the children. But they lived in their minds with him when he told of riding through a snowstorm to cross the Pecos River at Horsehead Crossing in 1883.

Arthur Francis Schnaubert served as foreman for the Holmsley spread in southwestern Upton County in the late 1890's. At the turn of the century he changed his position and moved his family from San Angelo to a dugout three miles south of Wild China Pond. His wife urged him to make provisions for a school, which he did. The cowboys converted a bunkhouse into a schoolhouse. Mr. Schnaubert equipped the school with blackboards, desks and school books. He hired at his own expense Miss Ruby Epps for the school year 1904-1905.[47]

III

THE ORGANIZATION OF
UPTON COUNTY

By the turn of the century, 1900, thirteen years had passed since the creation of Upton County.[48]

Within the 1,312 square miles there lay railroad land, public school land, Throckmorton Public School land and The University of Texas land.[49]

The population of Upton County in 1900 numbered forty-eight,[50] mostly cowboys and ranch hands. Only three families were living in Upton County in 1900. They were the Arthur Francis Schnauberts, the Frank Inghrams and the Jim O'Bryans.

Mrs. Bess Moorman in 1941 undertook to write a history of Upton County for a masters thesis at Sul Ross State College. She gathered much material from many old timers, but she did not follow through her original plan. She did make use of some of her research and wrote a "History of Upton County" for the *Handbook of Texas*, Vol. II, p. 825. Mrs. Moorman kindly gave me her notes in which she recorded her interviews with old timers. She recorded an interview with Cal C. Childress who left Glasscock County in 1905; he was in Stiles in Reagan County from 1906 to 1908, and at Upland in Upton County in 1910. Here he bought a blacksmith shop, and on December 26, 1911, he moved it to Rankin, the first establishment north of the railroad track. (Mrs. Moorman's research will be referred to as "Moorman Notes.")

By 1899 the Arthur Schnaubert family moved to the Billy Holmsley Ranch in southeastern Upton County. Here he had been offered a fixed salary, and he had the privilege of running his own stock and building up his herd. The family lived on this ranch for five years. The Schnauberts changed their location in 1905 when Mr. Schnaubert accepted the job as a foreman on the John R. Johnson Ranch in northwestern Upton County. It was with great courage that Mr. and Mrs. Schnaubert in their covered wagon moved their family to the new location and built a dugout for shelter. Soon after, however, with the aid of ranch hands, a passable house was built for the family. But there was no school for the children. The nearest school was forty miles away, much too far for the young Schnauberts. Ranch hands again came to their rescue. They converted a bunkhouse into a schoolroom for the children. The father proceeded to San Angelo, where he bought a stove, blackboards, desks and books at his own expense. He hired Miss Ruby Epps for the school year 1904-1905. But he was unable to obtain a teacher for 1905-1906. He employed Miss Lela Christy, aged 16, in the spring of 1906 for three months. When Miss Christy returned home, she carried with her $90.00, the entire earnings Mr. Schnaubert had paid her. The Schnaubert children were again left without formal schooling.[51]

Open range cattlemen in 1900-1901 were selling out their holdings above the Pecos River and in Upton County.[52] The State was taking a hand in an attempt to settle the open range with families. Railroads were being urged to sell their land, or it would be claimed by the State. Every time the railroads surveyed a tract of land for themselves, they had to survey a like quantity contiguous thereto for the State and number the blocks consecutively. The odd numbers were given to the company and the even numbers were retained by the State. The even numbered sections have since been given to the Public Free School Land Fund.[53] Much of the Railroad Land in Upton County lay within the open range. The land agents of the railroads in San Angelo and Midland promoted the sale of their company's land.

A. E. Stillwell and other associates, all of Kansas City, Missouri, on May 15, 1901, formed a company called the Orient Land Company for the purpose of buying, platting into townsites, improving, leasing, selling and otherwise disposing of land in the State of Texas.[54] Mr. Stillwell proposed to build a railroad from Kansas City, Missouri, to Topolobampo, Mexico, coming by San Angelo and passing westward.

The Orient Land Company proceeded to survey along the Middle Concho following the Butterfield Overland Mail Trail to Wild China Pond, Castle Gap and on to Horsehead Crossing.[55] Miss Flossie Coats, County Auditor of Reagan County, has said, "After a Stiles [Reagan County] rancher refused to grant a right-of-way for the Railroad to come through his property, the Orient came in 1912 through Spring Creek Draw and was routed westward." Like most of the rest of the Stiles people, Miss Coats and her family moved to Big Lake in 1916.[56]

In 1904 the drouth was broken by a slow rain beginning June 8 and steadily continuing day and night through June 9. The draws in the eastern part of the county below and above the Flat Rock Ranch filled with water rushing toward the J. M. Draw (Five Mile Creek) on the way to the Pontoon Crossing on the Pecos River. The water was so high at a windmill near the old swimming pool south of the railroad tracks that a calf lay drowned on the windmill tower, twenty-two feet above the ground.[57]

In the eastern part of Upton County, Ed Mosely, and his two sons, Matt and Jess, and a daughter, Mattie M., took up four sections each. Mattie M. Mosely was the first postmaster in Upton County at a post office called Mosely.[58] This office was established December 22, 1906, and discontinued June 30, 1908.

Henry M. Halff, son of Mayer Halff, who had been an open range cattleman, had a string of windmills from Pontoon Crossing on the Pecos River up the J. M. Draw to the Old Butterfield Stage Stand. Mr. Halff urged his cowboys to take up four sections of land each, with the understanding that he would buy them out. He needed range for his cattle and cowboys to take care of them. He moved his main head-quarters from Pontoon Crossing to the site across from the Old Butter-field Stage Stand near Dr. Elliott's rock house. Here, he believed he could get a good supply of water.

Mr. Dave Price, one of Mr. Halff's cowboys, related the experience of herding hundreds of cattle from the headquarters at Pontoon Crossing to Halff's new headquarters at the old stage stand near Dr. Elliott's rock house. On this cattle drive Mr. Price stated that the cowboys began moving the cattle at daybreak, driving them three or four miles to the next windmill, which took practically all day. By a week's time, they had driven the cattle to the stage stand. From here they drove the cattle to Midland to ship them "to the North," so said Mr. Price. The cowboys were delayed in Midland eleven days. The railroad facilities were inadequate.[59]

Halff hired the Engel Brothers to drill for water near the Old Stage Stand in what was then called the Middle Survey.[60] Halff hoped to develop an irrigation area to produce cotton, vegetables and other pro-ducts that would attract settlers to Upton County. He dedicated a site for a courthouse at Upland and advertised town lots far and wide for the price of a notary fee. The lots were quickly taken up by settlers, in-cluding the Schnauberts. To them it meant a chance to obtain a school for their children.

In 1908 at Midland, Texas, promoters were active in the sale of lots at Upland. They published the following announcement:

The new town of Upland (intended County Seat of Upton County) contains the only post office, school, church, stores and hotel within an area of a 100 mile square and is distributing point for all this vast expanse of territory.

Upland is the geographic center of Upton County. Two railroad surveys have been made through the County, the nearest being two miles of Upland.

Resident Lots in Upland $25.00
Business Lots . . . . $50.00 each
The Upland Townsite Company
J. A. Haley — President
F. F. Elkin — President Midland Loan, V. President
W. B. Elkin — Cashier Midland Natl Bank, Treasurer
S. O. Richardson, Real Estate Broker.[61]

Several of the settlers who came to Upland urged Mr. Schnaubert to circulate a petition for the organization of the county and the establishment of a school. Mr. Schnaubert rode from round-up to round-up and ranch house to ranch house for the signatures. He had the cooperation of Midland County officials who were overburdened with judicial matters due to the opening up of the Railroad and School Lands in the West.

The Midland County Commissioners' Court ordered a school trustee election immediately. Elected as trustees were G. S. Laughlin, R. M. Johnson and Walter Summer. They, with their neighbors, set to work to build a one-room schoolhouse. It was ready for use by October, 1908, when approximately thirty students were enrolled. By the fall of 1909, the school census justified the addition of another room and another teacher. This school term ran for nine months. Relief had come at last to the Schnauberts and their neighbors.[62]

Meanwhile real estate firms were being organized in Midland County. These firms were actively promoting the surveying of townsites and the sale of lots within the townsites.

On March 21, 1908, W. B. Elkins, J. A. Haley, S. M. Francis and S. O. Richardson, all of Midland County, platted and dedicated all the streets, avenues and alleys in the town of Upland, Upton County, as surveyed by R. E. Estes, County Surveyor of Midland County, for the public use.[63]

Six hundred forty acres—Block N, Section 13, Certificate 507, Abstract 243, of the H. E. and W. T. Railroad Survey — was designated as a townsite October 20, 1909. The townsite was named Bonita. The lots were sold to residents of Christian County, Illinois, most being sold on November 16, 1909.[64]

R. E. Estes, Surveyor for Midland County, for J. T. Barlow, who had purchased from the T. and P Railroad on February 2, 1909, ½ section 35, Block 38, had surveyed a townsite, called Heidleberg, on April 15, 1910.[65] Likewise, Greenwade City, Section 61, Block 35, H. & T. C. Survey, was surveyed by Bean, a surveyor, on July 6, 1909.[66]

Mr. Tyson Midkiff, associated with the town of Damron City from the start to the finish, more than a year later stated that he did not know why the town existed. In 1910 he and his older brother surveyed the townsite, located approximately thirty miles northeast of the present day Rankin. People began to move away in the fall of 1911, and Midkiff had the job of pulling the nails out of the buildings. "There was nothing to keep the people there," Midkiff said. He recalled that one of the town's promoters remarked, "If it hadn't been so dry, we'd have made a town."[67]

These townsite companies were being encouraged by an Act of the Texas Legislature, February 23, 1900, which required all the remaining public domain be awarded to the Permanent School Fund. The Act provided that as soon as practicable this land was to be placed on the market. A few so-called squatters began moving in with their families, their stock houses, their cattle, sheep or goats. This spelled doom to the open range.

The work of filing deeds and keeping track of the land business in the adjoining counties threw hysteria into the Midland County Clerk's Office. On February 14, 1910, the Commissioners' Court met to hear the petition of citizens of Upton County, which was attached to Midland County for judicial purposes. More than one hundred fifty signers of the petition of qualified voters asked the Midland County Commissioners' Court for the right of Upton County to be organized and function independently.

Accordingly, the Midland Commissioners' Court ordered that Upton County be organized and laid out justice of the peace precincts,, county commissioners' precincts and constables precincts. The Midland County Commissioners' Court designated the voting place for Precinct No. 1 as the schoolhouse at Upland with John R. Johnson as presiding officer, and the voting place for Precinct No. 2 at the Lee Breckenridge Ranch headquarters with Lee Breckenridge as presiding officer. The voting place in Precinct No. 3 would be at McElroy's headquarters with Dr. R. W. Cushman appointed presiding officer. The voting place for Precinct No. 4 was Jim O'Bryan's headquarters, with Jim O'Bryan as presiding officer.

The election was called for May 7, 1910, at which time all county officers and all precinct officers were to be elected to hold their offices until the next general election.[68] The voters would also determine the location of the county seat.

The officers had to make the returns to the Commissioners' Court of Midland. The following is from the *Minutes of the Commissioners' Court of Midland County*:

Be It Remembered that on this the 10th day of May, 1910, came on to be canvassed the returns of an election held in Upton County, Texas, for the purpose of locating the county seat of Upton County and to elect officers for said Upton County.

And it appearing that the following named persons and candidates received the largest number of votes cast at said election, it is therefore ordered and decreed by the Court that the parties receiving the largest number of votes cast at said election for which they were a candidate are hereby declared elect, to-wit:

For County Seat of Upton County, Upland, on Section 14, Certificate 3545, GC&SF Ry. Co. Grantee.

No. of Votes

For County Judge, L. W. Ainsworth 86
For County and District Clerk, R. C. Harlan 40
For Tax Assessor, P. P. Barber 50
For County Surveyor, R. W. Cushman 86

No. of Votes

For County Treasurer, R. M. Johnson 88
For Sheriff & Tax Collector, A. F. Schnaubert 60
For Justice of Peace, Precinct No. 1, H. B. Earnest 39
For Constable, Precinct No. 1, D. M. Price 6
For County Attorney, H. E. Webb 10
For Justice of Peace, Precinct No. 2, C. E. Shaw 4
For Constable, Precinct No. 2, J. A. Morrow 4
For Justice of Peace No. 3, W. T. Crier 6
For Constable, Precinct No. 3, Tony Damron 6
For Commissioner, Precinct No. 1, W. C. Summer 41
For Commissioner, Precinct No. 2, John Garner 7
For Commissioner, Precinct No. 3, Jeff P. Thomason 15
For Commissioner, Precinct No. 4, J. F. Lane 16
For Chairman, Democratic Executive Committee, J. Johnson . 35
For Democratic Executive Committee No. 1, W. E. Stephenson   8
For Democratic Executive Committee No. 2, W. O. Alexander   1
For Democratic Executive Committee No. 3, J. M. Sweatt . . 8
For Democratic Executive Committee No. 4, J. W. Harrington 13[69]

Mrs. Henry Earnest, who came to Upton County with her husband and three children in 1896, said the whole town celebrated May 10, 1910, by riding around the site of the courthouse in Mr. Henry Halff's touring car, the women and children riding inside and the men riding on the running board.[70]

The total population of Upton County numbered 501 in 1910.[71] An Upton County post office had been established at Upland, August 2, 1908, with Edmund D. Coatwright as Postmaster.[72]

Dave Price had staked out his claim to four sections of land within three miles of Castle Gap, and had married Annie Mills. He carried the mail to and from Midland, leaving Upland at 7:00 A.M. and arriving in Midland at 7:00 P.M., driving his two-team hack. Mr. Price returned to Upland by the same schedule the next day.[73]

Mrs. Price often rode the range with her husband until the birth of their child. She said that when her husband was away from home, loneliness engulfed her. She would go to the windmill and climb to the top just to see if her husband was in sight. Then she would watch for the dust, for that would be someone coming.

When court met in Upland, the wives of the ranchers would bring food for dinner. They also brought quilts which they had pieced. They put the quilts in at the Old Stage Stand where there was plenty of room and shelter.[74]

Mr. Halff built a hotel and general store at Upland. The store carried such staples as horse collars, nails, hardware, calico, beans, flour, sugar and all kinds of general merchandise. Also the store was a vault for money to cash the cowboys' checks. Soon after the county was organized,

Mr. Halff sold the store and hotel to John R. Johnson, who employed Dave Price to manage the store.[75]

The new school building of 1909 proved inadequate, and on June 12, 1912, an election called by the Commissioners' Court approved a $6,500 bond to build a new school building at Upland.[76]

New people had moved to the county. The Sheriff discharged the duties of Tax Collector, and his duties had been heavy. People who had titles to the land were living in other parts of the state or in other states. In some cases railroads had become extinct.[77] Mr. Schnaubert labored with the Midland County Commissioners and the General Land Office to determine a fair base for taxes. Finally, the Tax Collector wrote to the General Land Office that the field notes were so inaccurate that it was impossible to levy taxes on an equitable base. The Commissioner of the General Land Office authorized him to hire a surveyor to make new field notes. The Commissioner of the General Land Office accepted the new field notes.[78]

On June 22, 1912, an election was held to vote bonds to build a new courthouse and jail. Bonds amounting to $30,000 were to be approved or disapproved. $20,000 for the courthouse and equipment, and $10,000 for the jail and equipment.[79]

When on July 8, 1912, the votes on the $30,000 bond were canvassed, it was found that nineteen votes favored and six opposed the bond.[80] When the bids were let, the Court accepted the one of L. R. Wright and Co. of Dallas, Texas, to build the courthouse for $22,000.[81]

From 1910 to 1914 certain changes had taken place within the county, most notable of which were the establishment of a school and the organization of a county government and the establishment of its various branches.

The town of Upland had not developed as its promoters had hoped. The poor soil, the excessive summer heat, the recurring drouths and the inability of the residents to obtain water for irrigation caused them to drift elsewhere. The final blow came when the Orient Railway Co., instead of running its line up the Centralia Draw, ran it up Spring Creek Draw. Those who remained in Upland found employment in helping to build the railroad. By 1914 every family except the postmaster's had moved out of Upland.[82] Thus, four ghost towns are recorded by the General Services Administration, by the Upton County Deed Records or in the memory of the citizens of the county.

IV

THE TOWNS

Upton County during the second decade of the twentieth century was a place that tried the souls of men and women. Indeed, those who remained were compelled "to strengthen their stakes and lengthen their ropes." The population suffered a decline from 501 persons in 1910 to 253 in 1920.[83]

No longer did the people hope for the development of an irrigation project at Upland and in the adjacent four sections. The Engel Brothers had failed to find water in the Middle Survey,[84] but in the South Survey water had been found by F. E. Rankin.

The Orient Land Company sold on April 7, 1911, to the Kansas City, Mexico and Orient Railway Company the W½ of Section 24, land bought from F. E. Rankin.[85] And a townsite covering 215.77 acres was granted and dedicated on September 16, 1911.[86] Thus, the way was open for A. E. Stilwell to continue the construction of his railroad from Kansas City to Topolobampo, Mexico. Like Henry M. Halff, he needed men, women and mules to help with his project.

Many of the four-section farmers began leaving in 1911 and 1912. Cliff Newland, the windmiller for the McElroy Ranch in the western part of Upton County, remembers that their farm tools were left scattered over the county as a result of this exodus.[87]

By the fall of 1911 the railroad station had become not only the center of railroad activities in the county, but also the social and religious center as well.

In November, 1911, the Commissioners' Court ordered a road surveyed from Upland to Rankin. The road was approved February 14, 1912. The Commissioners' Court also requested Dr. Rome Cushman to survey a road from Upland to Midland.[88]

Upland's hotel and general store were put on skids and hauled to Rankin. The new name for the hotel was "The Orient." When the proposal was made to move the school, the remaining citizens in Upland and on the ranches in the northern and eastern part of the county promptly denied the attempt. By March 9, 1912, a post office was established in Rankin with Mrs. Opal Nix as postmistress. She served until February 20, 1924.[89]

On February 12, 1912, Ira G. Yates and others petitioned the Commissioners' Court for the creation of a common school district in the

Dr. Homer Power, physician and civic leader, established the first hospital in McCamey.

Dr. George Washington Elliott brought a thousand head of cattle to Upton County in 1883, and built a rock house across from Butterfield Stage stand.

An Easter Egg hunt in 1911 at the pump station, East of Rankin. The group rode in railroad cars. Those who can be identified: 1. Russell Bell; 2. Bill Huggins; 3. Laura Earnent; 4. Mrs. Bill Duncan; 5. Tommy Lee Stephenson; 6. Lela Earnent; 7. Mrs. Earnent; 8. Jo Lee Earnent; 9. Little Bill Duncan; 10. Bill Duncan.

Rattlesnake Butte, where the rattlesnakes den up.

Rattlesnakes being claimed by their owners.

Start of first Rattlesnake Derby in 1936, an event filmed by Fox Movietone News.

Rattlesnakes ready to race for cash purse at McCamey.

Arthur Francis Schnaubert and family. He was foreman on the Billy Holmsey Ranch at the turn of the century and later foreman on the Halff lands. He was elected first Sheriff of Upton County. In the photo are Mr. and Mrs. A. F. Schnaubert with Lola, Oscar, Tom, Johnnie, Edna, Lee, and Mamie Schnaubert.

The George McLaughlin family, pioneer ranchers of Upton County, in 1910. Photo includes George McLaughlin holding his daughter, Nina. On other horses are his sons, Guy, Ray, Joe Lane, Herman, and Lloyd. Another son, Bud, was born after this picture was made.

southeastern part of Upton County. The Court refused.[90] Not to be outdone by the first refusal, the petitioners again pleaded with the Court on August 15, 1912, for the creation of a common school district. Their petition was again denied.[91] But on April 23, 1913, the petitioners had the support of the majority of the voters, those who had put their houses on skids and moved them to Rankin, and by which time the Commissioners' Court likewise supported the petitioners and created all of the county in District No. 1.[92]

The first religious service in the county was held in Upland.[93] Of this service, Rev. Ira L. Parrack wrote to Mrs. Bess Moorman:

Dear Mrs. Moorman,

I had been preaching in the county for a year before there was a single church building in the county.

I preached in ranch houses and in the homes of settlers, I recall preaching at the Elliott headquarters on the Halff Ranch.

I also recall preaching in the R. C. Harlan home and remember that they had a daughter some 8 or 10 years old who had never seen a gathering except the old square dances.

That first spring (1908) I preached in that county, I killed more than 60 rattlesnakes, many of them with the rawhide buggy whip I carried in the buggy.

During the time I preached there, I was the only Baptist preacher in Upton, Reagan, and Glasscock Counties. I also covered the south part of Midland County; I preached 20 different places each month, and carried Bibles to sell, if people would or could buy them. But I would leave one in every home where they promised to read them. I left one in a home where the man said he didn't have any money and did not know when he would have any. The next month he told me of another settler who said he would like to get a Bible that way. Of course, I went to his home and when he promised to read it, I left one with him. That summer I held a meeting near enough for them to attend, and baptized both of the men and their families, and later got paid for both Bibles.

Your ex-pastor,
Ira L. Parrack[94]

The religious services were attended by persons of all beliefs, and there was no evidence of narrow denominationalism. When people moved from Upland to Rankin, the railroad offered the station for religious services, and church and Sunday School were held in the waiting room for several years. A Mr. Blanton was superintendent of the Sunday School.

On November 6, 1913, Mr. Blanton, J. H. Johnson and H. H. Russel started the building of a community church. Those who assisted them were I. G. Yates, the H. A. McDonalds, the C. C. Childresses, the R. C. Harlans, the W. E. Matthews, the A. F. Schnauberts, the J. W. Robbins, the E. M. Carruthers and Mrs. Mary Bell. The first person to unite with the church after the building was completed was Mr. I. G. Yates. He related that he joined the denomination of the first minister to conduct services in the church. As the minister was from the Church of Christ in San Angelo, Mr. Yates united with that organization. Sunday School was held each Sunday in the Community Church until 1932. By that time different denominations had been organized in Rankin. The Church of Christ was organized in the community church; the Baptist Church was organized in the home of Mr. and Mrs. Arthur F. Schnaubert; and the Methodist Church was organized in the home of Mr. and Mrs. T. F. Hickox.[95]

For fifty years these churches have grown and prospered. Other churches have been added. The Rankin Methodist Church commemorated its fiftieth anniversary June 25, 1967. Sunday School began at 10:00 A.M., morning worship at 11:00 A.M., and a special service at 3:00 P.M., at which time a special recognition service was held, including the consecration of the new building, the beautiful sanctuary and the education building.

Only a few of the charter members of the churches remain. But in their recollections, they remember the hard times from 1910 to 1920. They recall "the three-year drouth that ruined the range for cattlemen." In 1916, to save his investments, the old trail driver Schnaubert and his sons headed over 'Dobe Crossing on the Pecos toward the Rio Grande and into the Big Bend Country where the grass was green.

Misfortune overtook the father. Illness compelled him to return home for medical care and forced him to leave his stock. When his sons left Rankin to ride herd, they found the cattle so badly scattered that losses were unavoidable. Unable to meet the financial obligations because of this misfortune, Schnaubert surrendered his cattle in payment of his debts. His admonition to his children in these trying days was, "Always pay your debts; always tell the truth; always stay with your word."[96]

Likewise, the horse range to the south was hit hard by the drouth; Iona Poole writes:

During World War I, because of increased demand for horses in Arkansas, Louisiana and Mississippi, my grandfather and his sons stocked their ranches rather heavily. Unfortunately for them, there were early and late killing frosts in 1917 and 1918, and the rainfall was far below the average. These weather conditions meant no grass. Starvation faced the horses if they were kept on the range around Girvin. My grandfather heard there was a good range south of the Chisos Mountains and decided to move three hundred horses south of the Chisos, some two hundred miles away.[97]

Regarding of these hard years, we note the story of Mr. and V. G. Nevill, who had homesteaded in 1905 near an Eclipse windmill on the

Pecos River. In 1912 they moved to Dawson County to plant cotton. When the price of cotton fell to 6¢ a pound, it did not pay to hire pickers to take it out of the field. They moved their cattle to Gaines County in 1916, but a blizzard in January, 1917 wiped out their cattle overnight — 155 cows in one pasture. The animals were stacked on top of one another with their knees frozen down to the ground. Those that were alive had to be shot. The Nevills headed back to their Eclipse windmill on the Pecos. Mrs. Nevill took the reins and drove their wagon with their children and household effects, and Mr. Nevill drove their two horses.[98]

On April 11, 1917, a three-day slow mist began. Cattle froze in piles in Upton County. Cowboys cut fences to let the cattle drift to the brush. It was so cold the rain did no good. After the thaw set in, all the surviving cattle were shipped out; not a hoof was left in the county. This experience broke the little ranchers. Many of them went into the sheep business. The Schnauberts drove their stock to Brewster County to the 02 Ranch on the Terlingua Creek.[99]

Others who weathered these hard years besides the Pooles, the Schnauberts and the Nevilles were the Bells, the Carsons, the Christys, the Earnests, the Culps, the Hills, the Holmsleys, the Inghrams, the Lanes, the Monroes, the O'Bryans, the Robbins and the Yates. These people who had the courage to stay found a ready market for their horses, their sheep and their cattle during World War I.[100]

When the Orient Railway track was finished to Rankin, everyone in the country around came to meet the train as it puffed into the station. They accepted the engineer's invitation to take a five mile ride to the pump station and back.

The train furnished a means of carrying cattle to market, and ranchers no longer had to make a nine day trip to San Angelo. The train was a blessing. On the first Easter after the train came to Rankin, all the people planned to go to the pump station for a big picnic and an Easter Egg Hunt.

Besides picnics and barbecues, early Upton County settlers enjoyed rodeos, tournament races and dances. Dances especially were occasions for great merriment. They were usually announced several weeks in advance so that people for miles around might know about them. A dance usually began about 4:00 in the afternoon and ended about 10:00 the next morning. Friends and neighbors who had not seen each other for months had a wonderful time renewing friendships and relating experiences or discussing business. One group would dance awhile, then surrender the floor to another group, and on they would go. Music was furnished by fiddles and guitars.

Christmas was another time when the hospitality of the ranch was greatly in evidence. Several women would gather at a ranch house to prepare a great feast for their families and for all the stray cowboys and ranch hands around. Any stranger who might wander in was welcome.[101]

Through the solicitation and backing of Henry M. Halff, multi-millionaire of Midland and owner of the J.M. Ranch in Upton County, *The Upland Roundup* was established in Upland, the first county seat of the county, on September 16, 1910, by W. D. Riser, a young newspaperman in West Texas. With less than a dozen business concerns in the town and not many more citizens, the young editor rolled up his sleeves and pitched in to tell the world of the grandeur and wonderful opportunities of the new country and the (hoped for) new county seat. When the Kansas City, Mexico and Orient Railroad was being built out of San Angelo west, the residents of Upland "thought" they had a cinch on its building through this town, but they were doomed to the disappointment when the route was surveyed eleven miles to the South. The county seat was moved to the bustling little town of Rankin. So the people of Upland just bundled up their belongings and moved over, where in 1915 Mr. Riser established "the first newspaper in Rankin."[102]

By the summer of 1919 things were happening in Rankin that gave a new outlook to the few people who were there. Registered at the Orient Hotel operated by Mr. and Mrs. J. T. Holmes were a group of surveyors from the Bureau of Economic Geology from the University of Texas.

The engineers in charge of triangulation were Ralph A. Liddle and T. M. Prettyman; in charge of topography were D. D. Christener, F. D. Dodson and C. E. Bowman; and in charge of levels was Virgil Thompson. Others in the party were Ralph Hogan, Curt De Couser, Johnny Nichols and a young boy by the name of Keyes and another boy by the name of Collins.

There were no movies in Rankin at the time, nor any other means of amusement for this group of young college students who were eager for a pastime at night. They found a warm welcome at the Nix Barber Shop and Confectionery. The barber shop and tailor shop were in the front half of the building. The confectionery and the Rankin Post Office were in the other half, with the Nixes' living quarters in the back. This was the meeting place of the boys and girls of the town. There was a piano at the front of the shop, and D. D. Christener would bring his violin and play with a volunteer as his accompanist. Group singing took place. A great favorite was "Till We Meet Again," because the alto and tenor were easy to sing. This group of students seemed to be very congenial and loved their work. Coming in from their work, they related their experiences and often referred to the mountains and buttes in Upton County as if they were persons. They named them "Sugar

Loaf," "Table Top," "Rattlesnake Butte" and "Bobcat Hills." Their personal interest in their work was imparted to their hearers by this enthusiastic group of college students.[103]

Before 1922 the residents in Rankin had their own windmills to furnish their water. In 1922 Ira Yates drilled two wells and put in a water system for the south side of town. In the same year R. C. Harlan drilled three wells and put in a water system for the north side of town. In 1939 the City bought the water systems from Yates and Harlan. With the City's growth, they drilled new wells. The water was never palatable.[104] In 1953 the County issued bonds to drill fifteen wells and to sell water to the City of Rankin. At present the County delivers water into the city tanks, and the City takes over from there.[105]

When the Commissioners' Court denied Ira G. Yates and others on February 12, 1912, their petition to create a common school district for Rankin, they, no doubt, were aware of a school at Upland. Upton County contained many sections of University Land tax free. The sole support of the school depended on the ad valorem tax plus a miserly per capita allotment from the State Department of Education.

By 1913 most of the remaining ranchers in Upland had moved to Rankin and they outvoted the ranchers who remained in Upland. Although the Upland school continued until 1916, by the fall of 1913 the Rankin voters declared that the Rankin School District would include the entire county.[106] In the fall of 1913 not a house was available to accommodate the enrollment of the students. Work was rushed on the Community Church Building south of the railroad tracks. The children had no desks and only the equipment provided by two teachers and the patrons of the school. Enrollment increased so rapidly by the fall of 1914 that bonds were voted in the amount of $15,000 for the construction of a school building. The contractor, A. J. Olsen, had a brand-new red brick two-story building ready for occupancy by the fall of 1915. The trustees were George E. Blanton, president; J. H. Johnson, secretary; J. H. Phelps, treasurer; S. P. Pool and Ira G. Yates. They hired a man by the name of Maddox as superintendent of the school, along with his assistants, a Mrs. Mahaffey and a Miss Paul, in the first new building.[107] By 1916, 115 pupils were enrolled in the Rankin schools, so a fourth teacher was added to the faculty, and two years of high school study were added to the curriculum. Equipment was poor, and teacher turnover was high. Thus, it remained until 1927.[108]

Miss Annie Webb Blanton became State Superintendent of Public Instruction in 1918 and served until 1922. During her regime she initiated, among other things, (1) the passage of the Better Schools Amendment to the State Constitution, November, 1920; (2) a total advance of 51% in local taxation for school support; (3) a system of free textbooks and a plan for their distribution; (4) an increase in the State per capita tax from $7.50 to $14.50 in 1920-1921; (5) the policy of classifying and affiliating public schools; and (6) vocational work under the Smith-Hughes Law was greatly extended and improved.[109] This state-wide program served as a great impetus to small and large schools as well. It furnished a guideline for the older as well as the more recently created school districts.

One notable improvement in Rankin was the creation of a department of health of which Dr. Homer Powers (who came to Rankin in 1916) was the chairman. He insisted on the immunization of children against smallpox and typhoid fever and held his clinic in the school building. He received his help from the teachers in the building. Dr. Powers enlisted an interest of teachers and others in town in registering at the University of Texas for a correspondence course in Spanish, this move being a forerunner in bilingual studies in the school.[110]

During the first fourteen years of the Rankin school there were twelve different superintendents, with an even greater turnover in the teaching personnel.[111] One of the teachers, Miss Allie V. Scott, who came to Rankin in 1920 as a primary teacher and remained two years, recalled during her regime Superintendent Jefferson G. Smith. Mr. Smith set up the first permanent records of the school. A fifth teacher was added to the faculty, a four-year high school was organized and teachers' salaries were raised.[112]

In 1915 an election was held to change the county seat from Upland to Rankin. The change was bitterly opposed by those few in and around Upland, but they were forced to bow to the wishes of those who lived in the South Survey. The people of the South Survey were working on the railroad when they were not occupied by ranch duties. Since there was no courthouse in Rankin or the South Survey, the court records removed from Upland were kept in the upper story of the school building until 1923.

The people of Upton County voted bonds in 1923 for a new courthouse to which they moved all court records. It was well enough that they did this, for within three years the school enrollment had increased from 200 students to 500 in 1926. With all their failures and successes, the crowning glory of the ranchers of Upton County was their schools. They kept them going, by hook or crook, from ranch schools to qualified schools supported by the tax payers and the State of Texas.

From twenty-two miles away, A. L. (Jake) Henderson's roustabout drove as fast as he could to tell the driller, "The well's come in. She's heading big." The date was 2:00 A.M., October 28, 1926.

Yates No. 1-A, when it first came in, flowed at the rate of 450 barrels a day, but when it was deepened, it showed a potential of 72,000 barrels a day. Later Yates No. 30-A flowed 200,000 barrels a day — the largest gusher in the world.[113]

Although the Yates Field lay in Crockett and Pecos Counties, and although a total of 632 wells were drilled by 1966 with only 27 being abandoned, the field is expected to produce for many years to come.[114] Rankin became the unloading point of oil equipment for the Yates Field. The town has been active in oil field servicing and in truck convoys to the field.[115] Rankin became a boom town.

With the increased economic development of the town, a great demand for a medium of exchange followed. The Bank Commissioner, Charles O. Austin, a conservative, was reluctant to charter a bank in another oil boom town. However, July 1, 1927, he did issue a charter to the First State Bank in Upton County. The bank opened with a capital stock of $25,000, and the first president was the late John F. Lane. The first directors were John F. Lane, J. P. Rankin, George W. Newberry, Harry Baldwin, W. M. Noelke, T. J. Murphy and B. S. Taylor. Of all the original directors, only one is alive in 1970, J. P. Rankin, who resides in Rankin and who is ninety years of age.[116]

What did all this activity do to Rankin's school?

In September, 1927, H. G. Secrest was employed as superintendent on the condition that he achieve recognition by the State Department of Education of the school's classification and affiliation. When he replied that he could comply with the condition, he was given a three-year contract.

Because of the oil boom, many of the workers in the Yates Field and in an earlier field, the McCamey Field, lived with their families in Rankin. The children of these workers swelled the enrollment of the Rankin Schools so much that it was impossible to accommodate all pupils in one building; therefore, lodge halls and churches were used as supplementary classrooms.

The School Board gave Mr. Secrest permission to hire eighteen teachers to teach almost five hundred pupils. At the close of the school year in 1928, Mr. Secrest and his staff of loyal workers achieved affiliation in fourteen high school subjects.

With such a record, the patrons, in the summer of 1928, voted bonds of $80,000 to erect a new school building. Furniture and equipment valued at $25,000 were installed, and by the spring of 1930 the Rankin High School had earned twenty-two affiliated units.[117]

When a new oil field was discovered in East Texas in 1931, workers left the desert in Upton County for the new oil play. Thus, by the time school opened in the fall, only 237 boys and girls enrolled. The number of teachers was reduced to seventeen, and the school lost one and a half credits.

Mr. Secrest remained superintendent for fifteen years and laid the foundation for one of the most modern and well-equipped schools in West Texas.[118]

When the school opened on September 11, 1968, twenty-six years after Mr. Secrest's regime, 535 students are enrolled under the direction of thirty-nine teachers and an administrative staff of four. They are housed in three buildings with classrooms, one gymnasium, a beautiful auditorium and an administrative building.[119]

In 1952 the increase in oil revenue justified the application for a post office at Midkiff in the northeastern part of the country. W. L. Williams was appointed postmaster, September 16, 1952, with postal receipts listed as $5,046; he was followed by Mrs. Ida M. Hayden, February 15, 1955, with postal receipts of $5,612; and by Christine E. Upchurch, appointed March 9, 1956, with postal receipts of $6,757.[120]

Prior to August 20, 1925, George B. McCamey leased nineteen sections in southwest Upton County, on the E. C. Groom Survey, Block R, Section 8. McCamey drilled a well in the SE/corner of the NE/4 of said section 8 on the approximate date of August 20, 1925. The first oil was encountered in the well on September 27, 1925.

On October 10, 1925, Mrs. Minnie Crossett dedicated a plat for a townsite, Crossett, in Block 35, Section 23, H. & T.C. Survey. The Orient Railway ran through the site and served the ranchers with loading pens. J. Wiley Taylor was the attorney-in-fact for Mrs. Crossett.[121]

A post office was established in the service station on February 20, 1926, and was in operation until October 31, 1928, with W. F. Manning as postmaster.[122]

Three hotels, two cafes, a cleaning shop, a barber shop, several bootleg beer joints, a night club with a pool hall on the lower floor, and a gambling room on the second floor, one tank farm and a number of residences accommodated the people who came to this short-lived boom town. Today all that is left of this last ghost town in Upton County is the Texaco Bulk Station.[123]

The McCamey interests in the nineteen sections in southwest Upton County had negotiated with the Orient Railroad Company to lay a spur for the well. When the land man for the railroad learned the name of the oil operator, he printed the name "McCamey" on a board and nailed it to a box car on the spur. Thus, the town McCamey was christened.

The nearest place for purchasing supplies was the small town of Texon, forty miles to the east. Fuel oil for operating the machinery was shipped in tank cars by the Orient (now Santa Fe) Railroad to within four miles of the oil field and trucked the remaining distance.[124]

Judge O. W. Williams of Fort Stockton, a pioneer surveyor and frontier lawyer, spent an hour looking over McCamey, a boom town in its infancy. He found "Unpainted houses of one story with tin roofs, no lights and no water; narrow boggy streets crowded and congested; autos and trucks carrying lumber casing, oil and gasoline barrels, and household plunder." He stated that there were probably three hundred houses interspersed with lumber yards, open lots filled with casing and drilling tools, and restaurants galore.

The dust on the roads and streets three or four inches deep filled the houses and tents with dirt. Water was simply not to be found in town, either in wells or cisterns. Working in dust and dirty of face, hair and clothes, the average man must have felt that life in McCamey was hard.[125]

The McCamey Townsite Company was organized by Lon McKinney, Col. Brooks, Taylor Emerson, A. W. Caruthers and the Corpus Christi Real Estate Firm of Burleson and Johns the day after the well came in.

By the fall of 1926, McCamey had experienced its biggest building boom. Shacks sprang up like mushrooms on the greasewood flats. It was impossible to get a location on Main Street. It was estimated that more than 10,000 people resided in McCamey by the latter part of 1927 and early 1928. It was practically impossible to walk down the board side-walk for the throngs who crowded the streets.[126]

On December 13, 1926, an application to County Judge J. D. Patterson for the incorporation of McCamey was filed. Judge Patterson ordered an election to be held in the Public School House of McCamey for the purpose of submitting the question to the people of McCamey on December 27, 1926. The people voted to incorporate.[127]

Judge W. D. Riser published the first issue of the *McCamey Tri-County Record*, September 16, 1926, the city's first newspaper, which consisted of twenty-four pages. He edited and published the newspaper until 1929 when he sold it to Garland Adair, who changed the publication to the *McCamey News* after consolidating it with the *McCamey Leader*, edited by R. A. Hall. Adair published the newspaper until he sold it in 1932 to the Martin Company. In 1943 James Carll and Cuthbert Carll took over the publication of the *McCamey News*. When World War II broke out, Cuthbert enlisted, and after his return, he bought James' interest and has been the publisher since 1944.[128]

Even before the town of McCamey was incorporated, the water system was operating. The scarcity of water in McCamey from 1926 to 1928 was felt by the thousands of people who thronged the greasewood flats. The nearest source of water was Alpine, Texas, a hundred miles to the southwest. Water was freighted in over the Orient Railroad and

sold by trucksters at $1.00 per barrel. The scarcity of drinking water
was overshadowed by the lack of bathing facilities. Workers in the oil
field labored in fogs of dust and 115° heat. If they dived into the Pecos
River for refreshment, they invariably came up caked in alkali and salt.
The water system began officially at a meeting of interested citizens
February 8, 1927.

This meeting chose Dr. F. E. Gibbons, Mayor Pro Tem, and also a
Board of Aldermen. On February 28 the Board authorized J. S. Barlow
of Dallas, as consulting engineer, to advertise for bids to drill wells on a
location on which Mayor Gibbons had obtained an option. The bids
were opened by the aldermen on March 28. They awarded the contract
for drilling wells to Roy Irick of Plainview, Texas.

Mr. Irick drilled the first wells some four miles southwest of McCamey
within the Upton County line. The gyp water that he found so aroused
the citizens that they protested it was unfit to drink; it was also unfit for
fire fighting. It ruined pipes and pipe connections. The major oil companies proceeded to have wells drilled for their own camps.

The McCamey Chamber of Commerce appointed a committee of
citizens with G. F. Capps as chairman, and working with him were
George Ramer, manager of Burton Lingo Lumber Company, and Taylor
Conger. They were to work with the aldermen in their search for an
adequate and acceptable supply of water.[129]

George Ramer related that oil development in the Yates Field in
Crockett County south of the Pecos River created a terrific demand by
McCamey's oil interests for a direct road from McCamey to Iraan or
the Yates Field. It was necessary to go through the Tippett Ranch enroute. Thus it was discovered that good fresh water from the Trinity
sands could be obtained from a well seventeen miles south of McCamey.

Tedious negotiations ensued. Since the Pecos River had to be crossed,
Pecos County built a bridge over it. Mr. Tippett, after considerable
bargaining, agreed to let the recipients pay for a right-of-way and drill
a water well for his stock on the east side of the fence, in exchange for
a cash payment for water rights. The recipients were the oil companies
and the City of McCamey.

The Humble Oil and Refining and the Humble Pipe Line Company
furnished the surveyors to map out the road. Other oil companies contributed labor and supplies for fencing and for grading the roadbed.[130]
J. S. Barlow, according to the Minutes of the Board of Aldermen, was
employed on August 4, 1928, "to supervise the construction and prepare
the plans and specifications of the proposed water extension."

A few days later the sales engineer of the Lane Texas Company of
Houston, Texas, presented a proposal for drilling the wells and obtaining an adequate water supply. The Board of Aldermen accepted his

proposal. The Lane Texas Company completed the drilling of three wells: one 272' deep; another 285'; and a third 329' deep. Since this time four more wells have been drilled at this location. A report showed that:

McCamey is fortunate in having a vast supply of underground water. The water is pumped into a 100,000 gallon concrete underground reservoir at the well site by six turbine well pumps which vary from 100 to 350 g.p.m. in size. The water is then picked up by three centrifugal booster pumps and carried a distance of ten miles through two lines — a 10" cemented steel line and an 8" cast iron line to the booster station. The water empties into a 100,000 galon concrete underground reservoir and a 500,000 gallon steel ground reservoir. Here the water is picked up by three centrifugal booster pumps and runs through the automatic chlorinating system, thence into a 6" steel line and a 10" transite line for a distance of approximately five miles where it enters the distribution system and also empties into two overhead tanks, one 250,000 gallon tank and one 100,000 gallon tank.[131]

Through the efforts of the city officials, obligations of approximately $62,000 advanced to the City during the 1954 expansion program were cancelled by the Humble Oil Company, the West Texas Utilities Company, and the Continental Oil Company.[132]

Thus, in 1968, the 3,365 citizens (estimated 1967) of McCamey can enjoy a maximum daily demand of 1,372,000 gallons of water, 22.65 miles of paved streets, 51 miles of water mains and 736 miles of sewer lines.[133]

A post office was established in McCamey, March 5, 1926, with Amzi Caruthers as the first postmaster.[134]

The Townsite Company sold 25' lots for $100 each. People built shotgun houses, or used tents or cars with tarpaulins in 1926-1927. Each of three lumber companies obtained a right-of-way on the Orient Railroad. Burton-Lingo obtained a 185' lease on the railroad for unloading.[135]

Along the railroad were located the Atlas Supply Company, the Drane Humprey Company, the Frick Reed Supply Company, the Continental Supply Company, the Murry Tool Company, the Gulf Refining Company, the United Iron Works, the Parkersburg Rig and Reel Company, the Marion Machine Company, and the International Supply Company, all within three blocks along the Orient. Likewise, three blocks to the east and three blocks to the west were supply companies.

T. A. Ohlhausen drove the first stake to start the building program, November 18, 1925. He completed his building November 28, 1925. E. S. Dugan moved a frame building from Best. W. W. Beale began a building February 26, 1926. A two-story hotel was moved in from Best.

G. C. Pauley, Freight Agent for the Orient Railroad, was domiciled with his family in a railroad car on a siding at McCamey. He recounts the moving of a two-story railroad station from Owego, twenty miles west of McCamey. W. E. Russell recalls that he helped "crib" up the station to load it on two flat cars and move it to the site where the station stood until 1964.

In 1929 McCamey boasted eight automobile shops, two bakeries, four barber shops, eight hotels and cot houses, three cafes, thirteen grocery stores, six dry goods stores, six garages, two hospitals, eight physicians, four oil companies, four trucking and teaming contractors and three transfer companies.[136]

A Chamber of Commerce had been organized with H. L. Hildebrand as 1st vice-president, Leonard Proctor as 2nd vice-president and R. N. Morris as treasurer. The directors were George Ramer, W. D. Riser, Wm. R. Edwards, H. L. Hildebrand, W. E. Anderson, Leonard Proctor, E. F. Matejowsky, W. F. Matthews, E. D. Cozart, M. J. Johnson, F. T. Thaxton, R. N. Morris, H. B. Edwards and Sam A. Hall.

"The Hub of the Oil Fields" was located in Upton County on the main line of the K.C.M. & O Ry. Co. midway between San Angelo, Texas, and Alpine, Texas, the present terminus of the railroad. It is the nearest shipping point to the largest shallow oil field (Yates Field) in the world. While only two and a half years old, McCamey had a population of 7,000 people.

McCamey is the permanent location for two mammoth power and light companies, with an investment of four or five million dollars in equipment, serving West Texas, in addition to thirty oil well supply companies (only two less than Tulsa, Oklahoma), making it the second largest supply center in the world.[137]

The City of McCamey became the center within a hundred mile radius of such oil fields as Hurdle, McElroy, Santa Rita, Powell and Yates.

The Humble Pipe Line Company installed a 1,200 barrel refinery at McCamey that went into operation in March, 1927, utilizing crude oil from the newly discovered West Texas Fields.[138]

McCamey became an oil boom town on a belated frontier, in a region where nature was untamed and inhospitable and at a time when prosperity made difficult the hiring of men to work in such a region.[139]

The refinery burned to the ground in 1928 and was rebuilt the same year, with three hundred men employed. The Humble Pipe Line Company opened offices in McCamey in 1926 with the production, geological, and land and lease departments that were moved here from San Angelo in July, 1927.[140]

With Erle C. Bone, as president of the McCamey Business Men's League, great enthusiasm was generated over the celebration of McCamey's seventh anniversary of incorporation. That was held in April.

The League sponsored many events that appealed to cattlemen and oil men alike.[141]

An event that captured the interest of the public was the "Rattlesnake Derby," which was highlighted by a Junior Historian, Eddie Halamicek, who won first place in folklore division in 1952 under the title, "Slicker Slithers In."[142]

When in 1931-1932 oil fields were opened up in East Texas, workers left the McCamey area by the scores. Wells had to be shut down for the lack of help. Discontent was prevalent among the workers. Furthermore, the depression of the 1930's added more problems to the citizens of McCamey. Take the example of Mr. and Mrs. Dee Locklin, who wrote:

This is to certify that Mr. and Mrs. Dee Locklin moved to the Bobcat Hills area, located between McCamey and the Pecos River, July, 1931, with 2500 head of sheep, 1000 head of goats, 100 cows and 40 horses. This was an open range, making it necessary to keep the stock under herd, consequently, it was necessary to have organized drives against bobcats and coyotes to protect the stock. Gradually sheep-proof net wire fences were added. The State and the ranchers hired government trappers. Thus, was closed one of the last frontiers of Upton and Crockett Counties.[143]

Their son, Billy Locklin gives a graphic account of their experiences as follows:

The Great Depression of the 1930's broke many a man, but it made many another, one of whom was my dad, Dee Locklin. By 1930 he and my mother had hit rock bottom in finances. They had been ranching on the Edwards Plateau out in West Texas. Their lease lay in Crockett County between the Pecos River and Live Oak Creek. A better range would have been hard to find; good seasons with rains at the right times brought grass and weeds in abundance.

On one of their seldom trips to town they learned that prices on sheep and goats had dropped. Good ewes might bring $1.50; wool was priced at 9¢ a pound. There was no sale for goats or mohair. A cow with a calf by her side might bring $25.00, but there was not much demand for cows with calves.

From the Big Lake State Bank they had leased by the year a good range of 4,400 acres at 50¢ an acre. Since there was no market for sheep, wool, goats or mohair, it was impossible in the spring of 1931 for them to meet their obligations to the bank.

My dad mounted his favorite horse, Hoggie, and rode into Big Lake to lay the situation before the bank. His thoughts were grim. The bank directors were grim too. Of course, the bank was ready to take over the stock, and they could do that. But my dad argued that he wanted to pay off the note and that he wanted to keep his livestock.

After due consideration, the bank directors made a concession. They told my dad he could keep his livestock, provided he moved them to twenty sections of unfenced land three miles south of McCamey east of

Bobcat Hills. The country, the bank directors told him, had never run sheep and was literally alive with coyotes. He thought the deal over and said, "By golly, we'll go. We'll not give up."

The country gradually began to pull out of the depression, and the price of wool began to advance. The Locklins stayed on. Debts were paid off and life became more endurable. They did it once and it paid off. If necessary, they can do it again.[144]

M. E. Pittman, Superintendent of West Texas Utilities Western District, writes:

Most people who look at a map of West Texas find McCamey equal distance between Fort Worth and El Paso on U.S. Highway 67, and on the Panhandle and Santa Fe Railroad half way between San Angelo and Alpine. The principal assets wouldn't show on most maps: the prosperous people, the producing oil wells and the sheep and goats. The people numbered 6,000, the oil wells 900 and the sheep 250,000.

In a fifty mile radius around McCamey, you enclose approximately 2,000 producing oil wells, including the great Yates pool and three discoveries of the famous Ordivician strata. We have not overlooked the value of the livestock industry in Upton County.

Today all over the county from Crockett on the south to Midland on the north, sheep thrive and add much to the wealth of a county whose assessed value is $11,000,000.00. The superiority of wool produced in Upton County averages sixty-five pounds, while forty-eight pounds is the average in many sheep areas.[145]

Mr. Pittman was the first manager of the West Texas Utilities Company's McCamey office, whose job was to bring electrification to the oil fields. He arrived in McCamey, August 5, 1927. By the last of 1928 more than a hundred miles of high voltage line was constructed and in use in the Yates, McCamey and Powell Fields. He brought electrification to the West Texas oil fields and "with the same enthusiasm and vigor, he helped build McCamey, joining in every civic undertaking, helping to build the city of today out of the oil boom town of yesterday."[146]

C. M. Bender of Breckenridge erected the first brick building in McCamey in 1927. This building housed the Bender Hotel, the Bender's Department Store, and for nearly two years the McCamey Security State Bank.[147]

The McCamey Security State Bank received its charter No. 1549 on February 10, 1928, with the original stockholders L. C. Eastland, C. M. Bender, F. W. Holder, Howard W. Price, Tryon Lewis, W. W. Davies, M. T. Wilson, W. E. Anderson, W. A. Halamicek, H. M. Clark, H. L. Hildebrand, Wm. R. Edwards, G. W. Ramer, J. L. Schooler, W. C. Blanks, George B. McCamey and G. W. Fry. The original directors were L. C. Eastland, J. L. Schooler, W. E. Anderson, C. M. Bender and M. T. Wilson. The original officers were President, L. C. Eastland; 1st Vice

President, C. M. Bender; Vice President, Wm. R. Edwards; Vice President, George W. Ramer; and M. T. Wilson. The original capital was $25,000. On December 31, 1928, the loans were $4,674.35; the capital stock, $25,000; the surplus, $4,018.48 and deposits, $164,779.30.

The bank opened in the Bender Hotel Building, February 18, 1928. The opening deposits were $23,126.96. The opening capital was $25,000, and the opening surplus was $12,500. No loans were made for several months. The bank building was approved November 5, 1929. It was completed in 1930 and remodeled in 1949. The bank had very hard times during the first few years, but it was one of the few area banks which did not close during the Depression. In June of 1936 John C. Dunagan was elected president, and within a few years, the bank began to make progress.[148]

A leading West Texas newspaper has commented: "The citizenry must be credited to a marked degree for the progress in Upton County. From the rugged, determined cattle and sheep ranchers who pioneered the county, to the just-as-rugged and just-as-determined petroleum pioneers and their followers, Upton County has been blessed with the type of citizens who make West Texas great."[149]

On the corner of the Green Parrot Cafe in 1926 an itinerant Baptist minister preached to some who came to pray and to others who came to scoff. In 1927 Mrs. T. E. Baxter rounded up her young neighbors and armed them with sticks and pans. She told them to parade on the dusty streets, attract all the children who would follow, and bring all to her house, behind which the First Presbyterian Church now stands on Burleson Avenue. There she organized the first Sunday School and provided the children with literature from the Westminister Press. This was the beginning of McCamey's Sunday schools.

On its thirtieth birthday celebration, the City of McCamey stood in reverent attention while the following churches were recognized:

McCamey's Churches	*When Founded*
Hobbs Chapel, A.M.E. Church	1925
Christian Science Church	1926
First Baptist Church	1926
First Methodist Church	1927
First Presbyterian Church	1927
Southern Union Baptist	1928
Sacred Heart Catholic	1928
Church of God in Christ	1929
McCamey Church of Christ	1929
The First Christian Church	March, 1930
Assembly of God Church	1939
East Side Baptist Church	1951
West Side Church of Christ	June 29, 1951
Bethel Baptist Church	1954
Spanish Apostolic Church	1954[150]

Without schools, McCamey would have folded up. Early in 1926 the president of the Marland Oil Company saw that there were enough children of the employees of the company to make the need for a school imperative. Accordingly, he obtained permission from the State Department of Education to operate a school in the Marland camp four miles from McCamey.[151]

The Marland Oil Company bore the expense of constructing the building, operating the school, paying the wages of two teachers and for all the school supplies except the textbooks. When the school opened, seventy pupils were enrolled from both the field camp and the town camp. The term lasted nine months and it was the only term for the Marland Oil School.[152] Since all of Upton County was within the Rankin District, it was only after the Marland Oil Company obtained permission to operate a school for its employees that the Rankin school board began to make preparations for a school at McCamey.

Late in August, 1926, a four-room schoolhouse was built in the west part of the town. While the building was under construction, W. C. Williamson of Potosie, Texas, and three other teachers were hired. When school opened the first Monday in September, approximately 550 pupils were enrolled. The congestion was terrific. Three other teachers were secured as quickly as possible. Classes were held in two church buildings, a dance hall and a skating rink. Apple boxes and orange crates were used as desks. Only the barest necessities were available.[153]

The City Council in October, 1926, appointed Tryon Lewis, a Mr. Fisher, and F. E. Gibbons to present a prospective school district boundary, which the council had created, to the State Legislature.

From the files of the J. A. Phillips Company comes the following information:

The McCamey Independent School District was created by an Act of the 39th Legislature of the State of Texas, first called session, which was approved and became effective October 13, 1926. Provisions of the Act vest in the district all of the rights, powers, privileges and duties of a town or village incorporated under the General Laws of the State for free school purposes only. Such powers include that to levy and collect taxes, to issue bonds and to erect and maintain public free school buildings, control and management of the district is vested in a Board of Trustees to consist of seven members. Original members were Gilbert Sawtelle, J. T. Harvey, L. B. Guthrie, Tryon Lewis, Pat Schooler, Rankin Rudicille and F. E. Gibbons.[154]

On July 1, 1927, the citizens of McCamey voted bonds in the amount of $200,000 for the purpose of building and equipping a school building.[155]

At a meeting of the school board in May, 1927, C. V. Compton of Union City Schools in Tennessee was elected superintendent of the Mc-Camey Schools with W. C. Williamson the principal.

Fifth Street, looking West, in 1928.

A typical house in McCamey in 1926. Bernice Barnett is in the photo with little friend, Edna Lee Schnaubert.

Buffalo on the T. W. Johnson ranch were used to keep the "varmints" away from the sheep and to chase the hunters all over the rocks. Picture made in 1940.

Quarter Horse belonging to Tommy Johnson on the same ranch. The horse was named "Poco Yacca" and the picture was made in 1944.

Goats belonging to Dee Lacklin. One of many herds which were raised in Upton County during the 1940s.

John F. Lane and his daughter, Mabel Lane (Howard) at the "Y" ranch in 1930.

Upton County School in 1910. T. G. Clay was principal and Reavis Clay was assistant. Students included, the following: First row: Marion Woodmansee, Lancelot Ainsworth, Carl Webb, Bill Wyatt, Cook Williams. Second row: Charlie McLaughlin, Oscar Schnaubert, J. Lee Earnest, Herman McLaughlin, Lloyd McLaughlin, Uel Barker, Percy Johnson, Minnie Mae Johnson, Rachel Underwood, Beulah Taylor, Lady Gaines, Ruth Holcomb, Edna Schnaubert, Lela Earnest, Maudie Wyatt, Willie Mae Holcomb, Maurine Clay. Third row: Blanche Christy, Joe B. Johnston, Arthur Schnaubert, Frank Lane, Una Underwood, Myra Sumner, Georgia Mae Puckett, Gambol Riser, Marian Smith, Ed Schnaubert, Mamie Schnaubert, Teenie Barker, Lizzie Taylor, Reavis Clay, Guilford Clay. Fourth row: Lawrence Webb, George Webb, Mark Wyatt, Clark Faulkner (Puckett), Hazel Barker, Joe Lane. Fifth row: Ray McLaughlin, Delia Lane, Nannie Christy, George Underwood, Lena Schnaubert, Guy McLaughlin, Alpha Ainsworth, Willie Miller, Lee Schnaubert, Buck Underwood, Ethel Lane, Carl Underwood, Laura Earnest, Arthur Taylor.

Mr. and Mrs. T. G. Clay, Maurine Clay, Delia and John F. Lane. The Clays were teachers in old Upland School. When they left in 1910, they loaded all their possessions in the covered wagon and started for Fort Stockton. They spent the night at the John F. Lane ranch and this picture was made the following morning.

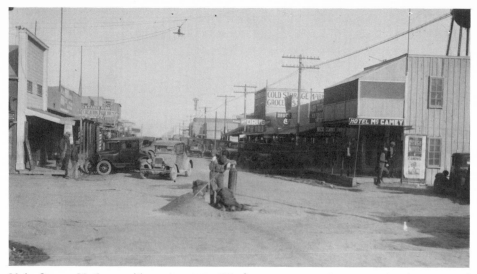

Main Street, McCamey, Texas in 1927. Workmen are removing a post in the center of 5th Street to which drunks had been chained as punishment.

Burleson Street, looking North, in 1928.

During the summer of 1927 Mr. Compton mapped out plans for the coming year. Salaries of teachers were high, and by the time school opened in September, Mr. Compton had procured a staff of thirty teachers with degrees. All children were classified basically by the Stanford Achievement and Otis Intelligence Tests. Those of the sixth and seventh grades and high school were placed in the new building, leaving the elementary and primary children in two old corrugated buildings, the Westover Building and another which was moved.[156] The student body came from twenty-nine states and three foreign countries. The students represented every type of home from that of a bootlegger to the most sedate and widely educated group that could be found anywhere, so the results from all types of tests and questionnaires were quite varied. Sixty-seven different religious faiths were represented, and there was not a single church building worthy of the name in which to worship.[157]

In November, 1928, additional bonds amounting to $150,000 were voted to build an elementary school building. When school opened in the fall of 1929, the building was ready for occupancy. Both new buildings were well furnished and well equipped, with efficient teachers working harmoniously together. The school was placed on the list of Southern Association of Secondary Schools and Colleges at the close of the school year. The school had received 38½ affiliated high school units.[158]

Mr. Compton's philosophy was "to train boys and girls into purposeful men and women. By their readiness to serve their fellowman can they realize the hopes of McCamey and attain the end for which the building was built."[159]

Perhaps no school system in the entire state has enjoyed the rapid growth that the local schools have in the story of the first seven years of McCamey's growth.[160] Because of the widely scattered oil camps from which many of the pupils came, it was necessary to provide transportation to and from school. Three buses were bought in the summer of 1928 for an expenditure of $8,500.00.[161]

Since the schools of McCamey — an even the town itself — came into existence because of the oil industry, it is only fitting that some of the oil companies in and around McCamey be mentioned. The Republic Production Company was possibly the first company in McCamey, followed by the Dixie Oil Company. The Marland came in the early days too, and established the first school. None of these three companies are in McCamey now. At the time of this survey, all of the school revenues are obtained from the following companies: Gulf, Shell, Humble, Stanolind, Continental, Cordova-Union, Sun, Texaco, and the T. P. Coal and Oil Companies.[162]

Mr. Compton was replaced by M. A. N. Blackman, who was head of the school faculty from July 1, 1933, until May 1, 1937, when he resigned. Mr. Howard E. Stoker accepted the contract to become Superintendent, May 13, 1937, and remained until June 30, 1951. He found a well-housed and well-equipped school and that Mr. Compton's philosophy had worn well. Enrollment had fallen off considerably, but the high standards of scholarship had been maintained.

During the 1930's after the oil boom died down, the local merchants saw the opportunity of maintaining a well established and permanent city serving as a supply center for the entire territory.[163] During the forties there was an increased demand for oil and gas as a result of World War II. New fields were opened up in Upton County, thus increasing the school revenue. Mr. Stoker, the superintendent of the McCamey Schools, backed by his school board and the citizens of McCamey, embarked upon a program for modernizing the teaching facilities. The old Westover School was stuccoed and converted into a Latin-American school. Dunbar was equipped with a new building and with new desks, maps and libraries. A band hall was built with practice rooms, and an auditorium, a homemaking building composed of all modern conveniences, and a cafeteria were added. Mr. Stoker also supervised the building of four teacherages with two apartments each and two residences, one for the principal of the high school and the other for the coach of the football team. A new grandstand completed in 1949 added much to the enjoyment of the community.

H. L. Wheat, who came to the school as superintendent in 1956, carried the expansion of building still farther. Three houses in the Pipe Line Camp were bought for faculty members. During his regime the football field has been extended as has been the primary building. A new physical education unit has been installed. The administration building has been erected. The old high school building erected in 1929 has been overhauled for a junior high school. On September 10, 1960, the citizens of the McCamey Independent School District voted bonds for a new $630,000 high school building,[164] which is beautifully landscaped and well equipped. It is the pride of the students as well as of all citizens in the district.

Aside from serving as the first high school building, 1929 to 1961, the building has served as McCamey's Community Center. In its auditorium, one has heard outstanding programs, sponsored by the school board of the McCamey Independent School District, churches, college concerts, clubs, the American Legion and political rallies. Here, also, weddings, funerals, draft board and food ration activities have taken place. The love and respect for the old high school building held by the staff of the high school annual expressed in their dedication of *The Badger 1961* shows the sentiments felt by the community and by many, many ex-students in many parts of the world today.

Truly the philosophy of C. V. Compton, the first superintendent, "to establish an organization of the highest order; to train boys and girls into purposeful men and women by their readiness to serve their fellow-man," has been well achieved.

The heart and the soul of the high school, the junior high school and the primary school are their libraries. The junior high school has some 3,000 books in its library, and the primary school some 3,000 books. The high school library has a total of 7,480 books, 260 phonographs records, 750 filmstrips, 7 sound projection films and 15 tapes.

Mrs. Bumpas, the McCamey high school teacher in literature in 1929, saw the need for organizing cultural interests in the boom town. In 1929-1930 she perfected the organization and the federation on the state and national level of the McCamey Women's Club. This club promoted the organization of a public library which today has more than 14,000 books on its shelves.

The Home Arts Club was organized in 1934 for the purpose of social association. The members have no constitution and little formality. They never discuss politics, religion or anything that might cause hard feelings. Of the fifteen members on the roll, only four of the charter members remain. They are Mesdames R. L. Brown, H. E. Cox, J. A. Haning and F. C. Reimers. They have made quilts for various orphans' homes in the area and for families who have lost everything in fires and floods. They often hold a Christmas sale of aprons, pillow cases and children's clothing.

Another cultural club was organized on February 24, 1953, and federated in April of the same year with Mrs. C. E. Watts as president — the McCamey Social, Civic and Art Club. It is federated with the National Association of Colored Women's Clubs in the Stokes — Parker District.[165]

Then, there are the American Legion and the Veterans of Foreign Wars, with their auxiliaries, the Independent Order of Odd Fellows and Rebeccas, and the Masonic Lodge with the Eastern Star.

On September 21, 1949, a group of twenty-nine women met to organize the Rankin Women's Study Club. Eight days later, the Rankin Women's Study Club met, adopted a constitution and by-laws and elected the following officers: Mrs. W. A. Hudson, president; Mrs. Jack Smith, vice president; and Mrs. R. O. White, recording secretary. The club was federated by the Texas State Federation of Women's Clubs and by the General Federation of Women's Club in 1949. The projects of the club have been the organization of a library, the conservation of our youth, welfare and fine arts. To achieve these, a reading room was set up which developed into a library. The Upton County Commissioners' Court set aside a room in the Upton County Park Building for the library and allowed in the budget a stipulated salary for the librarian and an expense account. The library has been enlarged twice. In the Conservation of Young People Project, a youth program entitled "The Conservation of Our Youth" was organized with the formation of a Youth Council obtained from the Commissioners' Court a room attached to the Park Building. The Rankin Women's Study Club has participated in all scholarships sponsored by the Texas Federation of Women's Clubs and in fine arts program, including painting and music. The club observed its twentieth anniversary in 1969.[166]

The Upton County Commissioners' Court authorized the establishment within the county of the Texas Agricultural Extension Service in 1935. The first Agricultural Agent was Casper Snell, who served until 1946. The first Home Demonstration Agent was a Miss Messek who arrived in 1940. Within the framework of the Extension Service, both adult and young people have an educational program. The 4-H Club work has always been outstanding in Upton County. Some of the ex-club members have made outstanding contributions to community life. Some are doctors, and a large per cent are in the agricultural field. As of 1968 the 4-H Clubs which are located in Upton County are in McCamey, Rankin and Midkiff. There are eighty boys and girls between the ages of nine and nineteen years of age.[167] Upton County has a 4-H Club Fair Grounds in Rankin and also a 100-acre grounds in McCamey. Another organization of interest is the Upton County Sheriff's Posse.

To keep our youth busy with worthwhile activities, the citizens became interested in Little League Baseball in 1952, and Nealie Moore organized forty-four boys in the League. In 1953 the boys came out with 32nd place in the nation. The boys took the Finals in 1955. A Baseball Federation was formed in July, 1956. The need for bigger and better facilities soon became evident, since the club was growing so rapidly. As a result, two of the finest parks in the country have been built on twenty acres south of the city limits of McCamey. In 1968, 210 children, regardless of race, participated in the program now called the Texas Teen-age Baseball League. Two Tournaments marked the summer's activities: the Freshman League and the Sophomore League. Rankin, likewise, has two baseball parks, and also an Upton County Park and a swimming pool.

In the 1930's an Upton County Park, extending three blocks across from the elementary and primary schools in McCamey, was built and it provided a swimming pool. A park and swimming pool were likewise established for Negroes. It is called the Dunbar Center. McCamey has two other parks: the Post Office Park and the Santa Fe Park.

Joining the Santa Fe Park is the Mendoza Trail Museum, which was begun in the 1940's by seventh and eighth grade students who were later organized into Chapter 76 of the McCamey Junior Historians. They researched landmarks and buildings for subjects for dioramas. The art work was done by a friend, Mrs. William Wolf. They completed a dozen dioramas in all. Their enthusiasm and interest progressed for some twenty years until both the county and the city of McCamey built a museum building, which has its own Mendoza Trail Museum Marker on Highway 67.

The Ed Kinney McCamey Teen Center operates under strict rules and regulations, rules that the teenagers have adopted themselves. They know that only by strictly adhering to these rules can their center continue. The members themselves enforce their rules. They do a very good job, a much better job than any adult or group of adults could do. They are learning the lessons of responsibility. They provide their own entertainment and recreation, making it clean and wholesome.

The Rankin Hospital and the McCamey Hospital are both county hospital districts. In February, 1966, an election was called for the purpose of approving the expansion of facilities.[168] The Rankin Hospital, organized in 1952, provides general hospital service and is equipped with standard hospital equipment and materials. The value of the hospital is $348,199, and the value of the equipment is listed at $90,696. In it are fourteen private rooms and three semi-private rooms, with a total of twenty beds.[169] The McCamey Hospital, approved by the State Board of Health, is a completely new structure costing $350,000. It includes twelve private rooms and eighteen semi-private rooms. It is fully equipped with an emergency room, a delivery room, an operating room, a recovery room, a laboratory, an X-ray room, a family room, and with TV's available. The hospital is a member of the Texas Hospital Association, the American Hospital Association, a Member Hospital of Blue Cross — Blue Shield of Texas and is approved by Medicare and Medicaid.[170]

The Upton County Historical Survey Committee, organized August 12, 1958, with the cooperation of early settlers of the county and interested citizens, carried out their objectives in celebrating the county's Golden Anniversary, May 28 and 29, 1960. The Survey Committee was convinced that the interest and enthusiasm of those in attendance at the dedication of the Upland Courthouse Marker justified the formation of the Upton County Historical Society. Four goals were established: (1) to compile biographical information concerning pioneers; (2) to enlist people interested in compiling local history; (3) to commemorate the past by placing suitable markers at various historical landmarks and sites; and (4) to open membership to all who are interested in carrying out the purposes of the Historical Society. The Historical Survey Committee has sponsored the placing of twenty-five markers at sites in the county. The second was a marker on top of Castle Mountain, in 1962 marking Castle Gap on a two-acre tract given by E. A. Schilling. On May 25, 1968, ceremonies dedicated a 100-acre park at Castle Gap given by the Caton Jacobs Estate. On both of these occasions one of the outstanding features was the performance of the Rankin and the McCamey High School Bands in rendering the *Castle Gap March,* composed by the Rankin Band Director in 1960. Clifton Williams, presently of the University of Texas Faculty, was commissioned to write this colorful, tuneful Castle Gap March by the Principal of the Rankin High School, Jim Mabry. Dr. James Day, of The University of Texas at El Paso, closed his Castle Gap Park Dedication with:

So there you have it. The heritage is rich and complete. Because it was a primitive geography, its beauty has been preserved for us to enjoy. The people of Upton and Crane Counties can be proud of this park on this historic spot. Castle Gap Park can become a veritable castle in the sky for those who love to look at nature's best.

Over the period of sixty years Upton County experienced high hopes, not all of which have been realized. From cattle and horses, then from sheep, the few people maintained a livelyhood. Then came oil, causing for a brief period boom towns, but followed by the Depression in the 1930's. Then again deeper tests were made in the 1940's, the 1950's and even the 1960's, which caused gains in the economy of the county. Much of the gains have caused the increase of better homes, better schools, the growth of churches and the well being of the county's citizens.

V

OIL IN UPTON COUNTY

DUST FILLED THE AIR as George B. McCamey drove his car up to
the porch of John F. Lane at noon on a hot day in June, 1925. John F.
Lane had been recommended to McCamey as being knowledgeable of
stakes needed to locate a site in the nineteen sections in southwestern
Upton County on which he had agreed to drill a wildcat well. A fast
friendship developed out of this meeting between the rancher and the
wildcatter.[171]

On September 3, 1948, George B. McCamey addressed a significant
letter in reply to an inquiry by Miss Pat Keffer of the McCamey Chamber of Commerce, McCamey, Texas:

Dear Miss Keffer:

I wish to acknowledge receipt of your letter of August 20, 1948, in
which you request information as to the Discovery Well in Upton
County and other data pertaining to the Discovery Well, and I will
endeavor to give you this information in order requested, namely:

1st.   Location of the Discovery Well was on the Baker Lands in the E.
       C. Groom Survey, Block "R," Upton County, Section No. 8. Well
       was drilled in the SE/corner of the NE¼ of this Section.

2nd.   The approximate date of the commencement of this test would be
       about August 20, 1925, first oil encountered in the well on Septem-
       ber 27, 1925, and was completed a few days later to a depth of
       2271 feet. The well was then shut down for about thirty days,
       then put on production and at the end of ten days was making
       about 40 barrels of oil per day. The Producing Formation is the
       regular Lime Formation, producing in this field.

3rd.   Insofar as I know the land upon which the Discovery Well was
       drilled, as above described, is still owned by the Baker heirs. As
       to the number of producing wells, I am unable to furnish, but
       can be obtained, no doubt, from the Railroad Commission at
       Austin, Texas.

4th.   As to myself, there is not much to add other than the fact that I
       am 23 years older at this time. I would like to add that as I com-
       plete this data for you, my son, Robert L. McCamey, is sitting
       across the table from me, and he was born on Sunday, September
       27, 1925, the day the Baker Well came in as a producer. In addi-
       tion to our son, Mrs. McCamey and I have three daughters —
       Virginia, Jacquelyn, and Georgia. All of our children are married,
       and we now have three grandchildren.

5th. The town of McCamey obtained its name in the following man-
ner: Mr. Clary of the Orient Railroad agreed at the time we planned the drilling of the Discovery Well to install a switch for our
convenience, at the present townsite of McCamey, providing we
would pay the cost of installation which we did, and the switch
was later named McCamey.

I believe the above information will pretty well fill your requirements
for information and I trust is the information you desire.

With kindest regards, I am
Sincerely yours,
George B. McCamey[172]

The 1920 Census recorded 253 people in Upton County. The next
year Carl G. Cromwell began drilling in Reagan County, adjoining
Upton on the east. Santa Rita No. 1 blew in two years later, May 28,
1923. Dee Locklin, still ranching in Upton County, was the tooldresser.
Plymouth Oil Company, as a holding concern by the Benedum-Trees
interests of Pittsburgh, Pennsylvania, financed the undertaking.[173]

Thus, the influx of population in the counties adjoining Reagan
County began. Mr. McCamey, after locating the site on his nineteen
sections in southwestern Upton County, began drilling about August
20, 1925. John F. Lane and Jim Robbins, ranchers in the area, dug the
slush pit. The tooldresser, Al Lindsey, the only survivor in the area,
says: "Right here is where it all started. It blew in with a gush and
started this oil field and the town off with a bang. Right after the well
blew in, this place swarmed with men, and there was work for all of
them in the oil-fields here."[174]

The land agent for the Orient Railroad, a Mr. Clary, upon learning
that oil had been discovered, instructed Jim Smith, the foreman of the
Orient Railroad from Girvin to Rankin, to construct a switch for Mr.
McCamey.[175]

Troop 31 of the Boy Scouts of America, sponsored by the McCamey
Lions' Club, erected a marker at the site of the well in the spring of
1932. As an eighth-grader, J. C. Tennyson, in 1955 constructed a diorama
of the discovery well with the old bull wheel and other remains around
it. Mr. McCamey and his associates sold the Baker No. 1 in 1930,[176] but
the sale of the discovery well did not end his interest in the town of
McCamey. He returned for every birthday celebration of the town until
his death. His generosity was extended in the many facets of life in and
for the town. On one occasion when he was approached by a leader of
the Girl Scouts, Mrs. George Ramer, who explained to him that the
Permian Basin Council was seeking to buy the Mitre Peak Ranch for a
campsite for the G.S.A., Mr. McCamey gave $500 for this struggling
project.[177]

The Republic Production Company, the Dixie Oil Company and the Marland Oil Company — the latter established the first school in Mc-Camey — were leading operators in the McCamey Field. They had sold out by 1944. So a major part of the school revenue was and is obtained from the Gulf, Shell, Mobil, Stanolind, Continental, Cordova-Union, Sun, Texas Pacific Oil, Humble Oil and Refining and the Humble Pipe Line Companies.[178] These early fields flanked King Mountain to the eastward for eleven and one-half miles.

The Humble Pipeline and Production Company began leasing the right-of-way in 1919; they filed December 18, 1926, for the purchases for right-of-way for oil, gas, water or whatever they needed the land for. In 1927 they bought from Burleson and Johns the south part of Section 65, Block 35, of the H. & T.C. Survey, where they established a division office and an Employees Community and Recreation Hall.[179]

In January of 1929 Humble contracted with Mr. and Mrs. V. G. Nevill for their pump station in Section 74 in Pecos County to supply water for the Humble Production Camp and the Humble Refinery.[180] Amos Floyd and Arthur Caldwell II supervised the joining of the pipe.[181]

In his remarks at the dedication of the historical marker of the Humble McCamey Campsite, L. H. Byrd said:

Humble started limited drilling and operations soon after the discovery of the McCamey Well in 1925. By 1926 Humble's operations had reached such a tempo that a refinery was built, and a major pipeline was started to carry oil from the Basin Area to Ingleside on the Gulf of Mexico. It was here in 1927 that Humble's production department created a major operating headquarters and employees community. It was here that the company's sales department opened marketing facilities in the area, building bulk and service station outlets to serve the expanding oil industry and the thousands of car owners in the new and busy communities, which grew a pace with the development of oil fields.

The original McCamey campsite was a 32.5 acre tract which was purchased March 24, 1927, and a 100 acre tract was added shortly thereafter. The original refinery went into operation in early 1927 but burned soon after. It was rebuilt by the end of the year. At one time over 300 employees worked at the refinery.

Humble Pipe Line Company employees moved into the camp as did production, geologic and land departments. Originally, twenty-five company houses were built, and bunkhouses and mess halls were added.

In 1930 Humble purchased additional houses from Marland Oil Company about the time Marland became a part of the Continental Oil Company.

In 1935 the Humble moved its West Texas headquarters to Midland, from which point it continues to serve as headquarters in West Texas today.

When the oil boom diminished at McCamey, its visionary merchants and citizens saw the opportunity for a permanent city to serve as a supply area of that part of West Texas.[182]

On this same occasion Mayor B. A. Epley of McCamey stated that the Humble Companies have played an important part not only in the beginning of our city, but they have been a tremendous help to this community throughout the years.

In 1954 the Humble Companies contributed to the improvement of the city water system by donating more than $200,000 in material and money, and again in 1957 the same company donated five miles of 6" water line to the City. Humble was initially responsible for our beautiful Santa Fe Park. Mayor Epley concluded: "I want to take this opportunity to say, 'Thank you,' to the Humble Companies."[183]

In 1927 the Humble Companies furnished the town of McCamey a surveyor for laying out the road from the Yates Field to McCamey. This road passed through ranches whose owners consented to sell the right-of-way, provided a wolf-proof fence would be built along it. The various oil companies furnished materials and laborers to comply with the ranchers' requirements. Eighteen months were needed to complete the job, according to George Ramer, President of the McCamey Chamber of Commerce in 1927. Mr. Ramer recalls this project of the Chamber as one of its most outstanding accomplishments. The chairman of the project was G. F. Capps, with George Ramer, H. L. Hildebrand, Taylor Conger and Col. F. A. Hornbeck[184] working with the Commissioners' Courts of Crockett and Pecos counties, and with ranchers as well. The Commissioners' Court of Pecos County authorized a bridge across the Pecos River on the road to McCamey and another across the river toward Rankin.

The Humble Companies have contributed not only to the economic well-being of McCamey, but they have contributed to the cultural aspect as well. In 1961 when the McCamey Women's Study Club made a study of the history of Upton County, upon their request the companies sent a representative with an art exhibit to be displayed in the Upton County Park Building. Many of the paintings were the work of Buck Schiwetz. In addition, Cecil Gill, an employee in the Geophysics Research Department and an expert craftsman in wood, made a relief map of Upton County for the children of the public schools to be displayed in the Mendoza Trail Museum. This map was mounted according to Mr. Gill's specifications by the industrial shop of the McCamey School System, under the direction of J. W. Vaughn. The map has attracted the attention of children from towns near and far, as well as the general public.

For the Mendoza Trial Museum, Michael L. Benedum advised W. J. Grissett of the Midland office of the Plymouth Oil Company to present two bit gauges which had been used in drilling Ellenburger wells at Texon. These wells were the deepest in the 1920's at the time these gauges were used. The 27-inch standard tool gauge was the largest used, and the 3⅜-inch gauge was the smallest used in these wells. Mr. Grissett delivered the gauges to the museum December 15, 1956.

Mr. Grissett wrote the museum that there were other items of interest at the Plymouth office in Texon; and on January 13, 1957, Junior Historians Arthur Caldwell III and Charles Cregg went to Texon, where they interviewed C. M. Satterwhite of the Plymouth Oil Company. He gave to the Mendoza Trail Museum on behalf of Mr. Benedum and the Plymouth Oil Company the following items: shale and other fossils from the first wells in the Texon area; a tool to knock the water course out of a large drill bit; a spudding shoe that was used in the Santa Rita No. 1; a never-slip tool and rope for running casing by hand, which was probably used on Santa Rita No. 1, but certainly on the first wells of the area; a Meyers low-down hand pump used on the first wells, commonly called among oil field workers, the "one-arm Johnny" and "armstrong"; numerous cores and samples from formations of the first wells in that area; and a large 5-shelf cabinet with glass doors, in which are housed the fossils, cores and formation samples donated by the Plymouth Oil Company.[185]

Mr. Benedum organized the Plymouth Oil Company as a parent company for the Big Lake Oil Company. He hoped that Plymouth would be one of the major operators in West Texas, and his dreams became a reality. He started the flow of oil not only on the University of Texas Lands, but his capital also opened the door to the Great Permian Basin, of which more than two millon acres are owned by the University of Texas.[186]

Mike Benedum had employed Levi Smith twenty-six years prior to the Big Lake discovery. Of him, Mike said, "He is as honest as the day is long. He will watch every penny, and he does not have to be watched." Levi Smith was elected president of the Big Lake Oil Company and established his offices in San Angelo and Big Lake. He supervised all operations in the area for Mike Benedum and his associates.

It was the same Levi Smith to whom Ira Yates had often appealed to drill on his land. Since Yates had seen oil in the limestone pockets on his ranch, he wanted Levi Smith to drill. Yates trusted Smith and wanted no one else to drill; Mr. Smith finally consented to drill on the Yates Ranch, even if he had to drill the well himself.

Through Mike Benedum, Levi Smith obtained a big block of the Yates area for the Mid-Continent Oil and Gas Company, with this company holding the Yates lease. Transcontinental Oil Company was a Benedum Company, and Mid-Kansas had once been a Benedum unit but at that time (1926) was a subsidiary of the Ohio Company. Transcontinental and Mid-Kansas had a working agreement to drill a few

test wells in the area. Smith reminded Benedum of his promise to Ira
Yates. Benedum induced the Ohio Company to go in with him in drilling
a well on the Yates Ranch.

Drilling began on October 6, 1926, and the well blew in with a mighty
roar on the night of October 28, 1926. The Yates Field became one of
the most spectacular in West Texas. It consisted of 20,000 proved acres,
with a potential of 40,000 barrels to the area and contained several wells
that, if unrestricted, might have a flow of 100,000 barrels a day.

In 1939 Mr. Benedum's Plymouth Oil Company acquired several
blocks of acreage where Upton, Midland, Glasscock and Reagan Counties join. In 1940 Mr. Benedum insisted the company begin drilling
Alford No. 1 in Upton County. The drilling was suspended after a year
because the chert through which the bit was passing was too hard for
the equipment that was then available.[187]

Mr. Benedum never forgot the Alford No. 1. By 1947 diamond drills
had been developed which could cut through flinty rock. Mike arranged
with Mr. Fred Turner, an independent operator in Midland, to complete
the well. Turner gave up on the job because of the peculiarities of the
formations and the great gas pressure. He turned Alford No. 1 over to
Tom Slick, another independent operator, who completed the well.[188]

Mr. Benedum followed the progress of the drilling by telephone. His
persistence and determination are largely responsible for the early completion of Alford No. 1. The Benedum Field spreads twenty-one miles
in every direction from the corner of Upton, Midland, Glasscock and
Reagan Counties.[189]

By October, 1954, eighteen hundred wells had been drilled in this
area. The Plymouth Oil, Phillips Petroleum, Texas Natural Gas and the
El Paso Natural Gas Companies had huge plants in this area. They had
pipelines running to the Benedum Spur of the Santa Fe Railroad tied
into the Panhandle and Santa Fe at a point ten miles due east of Rankin,
Texas. Many more miles of pipeline carried crude oil, gas, butane, propane and butadiene from the plants and the field to all parts of the
country.

The result of Mike Benedum's wildcatting in the Permian Basin
was that minor and major oil companies continued to explore and to
drill, much of their activities on lands of The University of Texas and
the Texas Public Schools. It is difficult to realize that thirty-three years
ago Mike Benedum's faith in oil in West Texas produced the Big Lake-
Texon, the Yates and the Benedum fields.[190]

E. G. Rodman and W. D. Noel, drillers, were veterans in the oil business as early as 1940. They opened up the Rodman-Noel Oil Field with
Radford Grocery No. 1 located from the south and west lines of Section
1 of the Gulf Colorado and Santa Fe Survey in Railroad Commission

District 7 C, January 13, 1953. This well had a natural flowing potential
of 960 barrels in twenty-four hours from the Grayburg foundation at a
total depth of 1,744 feet. The Rodman-Noel Field has a number of wells
completed for a natural potential in excess of 3,000 barrels a day. The
opening of this field contributed substantially to the 1925-1960 Upton
County total of 272,628,476 barrels of production.[191] The Weir No. 1 Oil
Well was drilled in by Brahaney Drilling Company in 1961. It was discovered by E. G. Rodman, W. D. Noel and the El Paso Natural Gas
Company. This well was the first quadruple completion in West Texas
and was called by the American Association of Petroleum Engineers the
most important development of the year 1961. It was the most prolific
discovery in many years, drilled to a depth of 12,432 feet. It produces
from the Upper, Middle and Lower Strawn Zones and from the Bend.
Rodman and Noel have been responsible for numerous significant discoveries in the Permian Basin of Texas and New Mexico and have led
in the establishment of a vast petro-chemical complex in Odessa which
utilizes petroleum by-products once scrapped as waste in the making of
such things as plastics. Such leadership and such wells as Weir No. 1
have enabled Upton County for many years to be one of the outstanding
production areas in Texas.[192]

Plants of the El Paso Natural Gas Company in Upton County are the
Wilshire Plant in Block E, Section 135, CCSD&RGNG Survey; the Benedum
Plant in Section 50½, P. B. Scott Survey; the Pembrook Plant in Block
X, Section 1, the Dewitt Survey; the Sweetie Peck Compressor and
Treating Plant, Block 41, Section 20, T&P T5S Survey, together with
pipelines, telephone and microwave equipment in all plants.[193]

The Shell Oil Company, actively engaged in drilling in Upton County,
has very generously given a collection of named oil well cores to the
Mendoza Trial Museum. Besides this, their public relations department
has photographed the Benedum Campsite Marker. The Upton County
Tax Rolls designate, according to the 1968 valuation based on 20% valuation, is $1,132,670.00.

Other large fields in Upton County based on 20% valuation include:

King Mountain Field	$1,394,620.00
The McCamey Field	1,525,590.00
Sprayberry Field	3,240,450.00
Wilshire Field	5,436,400.00
Amacker-Tippett Field	5,835,710.00
McElroy Field	8,003,250.00
Pegasus Field	10,347,640.00[194]

The many small operators in the oil industry in Upton County maintain an interest that offers much to the folklore of the industry as is

recorded in books and magazines. Howard Wolf recalls that in February, 1942, his father, William Wolf, sub-leased from the Shell Oil Company three wells. Howard spent one summer on the leases with his uncle and aunt, and he recounts the experiences of a small boy winning fourth place in folklore in the Junior Historian Writing Contest.[195]

A citizen of McCamey who arrived in August, 1935, during the Depression, has distinguished himself by his many benefactions to the town. He is Claude W. Brown. Two months after Brown's arrival, his wife and daughter joined him. Until 1937 they lived in an apartment at the Texas Hotel, operated by Mother Perle Harris. By 1937 he was able to trade for the old Continental Station on Highway 67. This he converted into an apartment at the rear and a place of business at the front, in which he sold oil-field equipment. By 1941 he was able to buy oil leases around Crane and McCamey. Later in 1946 he acquired another sideline — some drilling rigs in Crockett County. Another business interest developed through a conversation with County Judge W. R. Edwards, owner of the Chevrolet Motor Company, when Judge Edwards casually remarked that for a little he would sell the motor company. Mr. Brown quickly replied, "And for a little I would buy it." This he did and the next day the deal was closed. Mr. Brown dealt in war surplus pipe, while through 1950 he was running his drilling rigs and contracting. He acquired a son-in-law, E. W. Thorp, and soon they formed the Brown and Thorp Drilling Company. They opened a field near Girvin, Texas (Pecos County), and drilled seventy-two wells. They sold out in 1954 for $2,000,000 and in 1957 acquired one hundred thirty wells at Borger. There they sold out within thirty days for $5,000,000. They now have in production something over a hundred wells in this area. Mr. Brown's belief in the area led to his leasing a 17,000-acre tract from the Tippett-Amacker Estate for fifteen years, on which he runs sheep and cattle. Those who have lived in this area from 1935 to the present are aware of the many benefactions of Claude W. Brown. He has given acreage for the construction of churches and lodges and is responsible for private benefactions.[196] *The 1967 Upton County Tax Record* shows that Mr. Brown owns 1327 acres of land around McCamey; 405 city lots in McCamey; and a royalty interest in 24 sections within Upton County.[197]

The fabulous McElroy Oil Field was opened up in Crane and western Upton Counties in 1926. In the same year Mike Benedum returned to drill in a wildcat on the Yates Ranch in Pecos County. He came back a third time in 1947 to open up the Benedum Field in Northeastern Upton County. And in the same year in southern Midland and northern Upton Counties, the Pegasus Field was opened up. Upton County accounted for a crude production of 18,426,100 barrels in 1965, bringing its total to 345,247,100 barrels since discovery by George B. McCamey in 1925.

Oil production in 1966 reached 363,673,200 barrels.[198] By no means is the oil industry limited to the production of crude oil. Plants within Upton County have been erected to produce by-products, a few of which are butane, propane, butadiene, gasoline and ethane. They have a value reaching into seven and eight figures.[199]

Bank deposits in Upton County, as of December 31, 1964, amounted to $6,982,000 with assets of $7,944,000.[200]

Major oil companies, as well as independents, have participated in the development of the industry within the county. Their taxes have helped build schools, libraries, museums, hospitals and churches. They have likewise supported the development of roads and parks.

The keystone of the arch of the boom town and the old town alike that survive is their schools. The tax men of the oil companies are the last to limit the resources that are needed for the construction and maintenance of good schools.[201]

VI

BIOGRAPHIES

THE BIOGRAPHIES THAT FOLLOW reflect the warmth of grandchildren, children, wives, friends and those who did research of records of people from Alsace-Lorraine, Germany, and from many states in the United States. The stories tell how Upton County's primitive geography has been transformed into one of the counties laden with riches.

"From that era a new and progressive one has come to Upton County with a population now of 6,239. No longer are the trails impassable — they are gleaming strips of pavement. No more standard rigs, no more cable tools with steam boilers; instead there are beautiful rotary rigs with massive diesel engines, ablaze at night with many lights. The sweeping valleys, even the high mesas, are now thickly dotted with pumping units, tank batteries and drilling wells. Only the tint in the sky at dawn and the evening shadows on the mesas remain unchanged."
— Olive O. (Mrs. George B.) McCamey, January 30, 1968.

BENEDUM, MICHAEL LATE

Mike Benedum, the son of Emanuel and Caroline Southworth Benedum, was born in Bridgeport, West Virginia, July 16, 1869. His marriage to Sarah Nancy Lantz of Blacksville, West Virginia, in 1896, marked the beginning of his spectacular career. In their fifty-five years together they participated actively in the work of the Methodist Church and Benedum Hall. They regarded surplus wealth as a sacred trust to be shared with their fellowman. The Claude Worthington Benedum Foundation, a Pennsylvania non-profit corporation, was organized in December, 1944, as a memorial to their son, Claude, who died of influenza during World War I while serving in the Chemical Corps of the United States Army. Under Mrs. Benedum's will the foundation received 5½ million dollars. By July 30, 1959, the date of his death, Mr. Benedum had given the foundation $1,090,450, and by his will, he gave the foundation one half of his residual estate.[202]

In the sixty-nine years of his spectacular career, Mr. Benedum was engaged in the production, refining, transportation and marketing of oil. The Great Wildcatter, with his partners, made successful strikes in Illinois; the Caddo Field in Louisiana; Tuxpam Field in Mexico; the

The presentation of the Map of Upton County was made by Cecil Gill of Humble Oil and Refining Company. Present for the event were Floyd Bushwar, N. Ethie Eagleton, Mr. Nevinger, Mrs. John Summerall, Cecil Gill, Arthur Coldwell II, C. W. Brown, Durwood Langston, Mrs. Arthur Caldwell II, and C. G. Forrester.

Monument erected by Troop 31, Boy Scouts of America, at the site of Baker No. 1, the discovery well in the McCamey oil field. The monument was completed in 1931.

Harris Machine Shop in 1934. In the photo are Shorty Phillips, Wilbur Harris, and E. E. Miliron.

McCamey Pipe and Supply Company, operated by William Wolf, helped to supply pipe and fittings for oil drilling.

Mrs. Wilbur Harris and son, Leon, with the first Model "A" Ford sold by Hildebrand Motor Company in McCamey in 1928.

The Upton County Historical Society at the dedication of a marker at the courthouse. Pictured are Miss Maggie Taylor, Mrs. Jack Smith, Mrs. E. C. Higday, Mrs. Ann Clark, Mrs. George Ramer, Mrs. William Wolf, Mrs. Opal Rix, and Miss N. Ethie Eagleton.

The Pecos River flooded its banks, went on the rampage in 1930. Old Girvin Bridge was almost covered.

Eagle Scouts, McCamey County in 1956. Standing are Dale Reynolds, Parry Walden, Tex Lucas, Dwaine Eubanks, Jerry Floyd, David Crawford, and Robert Adams. Seated are N. Ethie Eagleton, Ed Kinney, Amos Floyd, and Bill Ramsey.

McCamey Cub Scouts with their leaders, Dan Cook and Cecil Gill, include Robert Wayne Hayes, Lonnie Gunter, Darrel Lowe, and David Thompson. The group inspected a relief map of Upton County.

deMares Field in Columbia, South America; the Desdemona; the Big Lake; the Yates; the East White Point; and later the Benedum, the Susan Peak and the Benavides Fields, all in Texas.[203]

Within three years' time, with the leadership of Mr. Benedum, the Yates Field became the richest field in the United States. Its production became so prolific that the idea of proration was ushered in Texas. The Yates' operators asked the Texas Railroad Commission on May 31, 1928, to adopt proration rules to govern the Field, and on June 20th, the Commission issued such orders.[204]

In 1939 Mike Benedum's Plymouth Oil Company acquired several blocks of acreage at the intersection of Reagan, Glasscock, Midland and Upton Counties. At his insistence in 1940, the company began drilling the Alford No. 1 in Upton County. The operation was suspended after a year's drilling because the chert through which the bit was passing was too hard for the equipment then available.

Mike Benedum never forgot Alford No. 1. By 1947 diamond drills had been developed which could cut through flinty rock found in the hole of Alford No. 1. Benedum arranged first with an independent operator, then finally with Tom Slick, who carried the drilling through to completion. Mr. Benedum followed the drilling through by telephone. By his persistence and determination he was responsible for the early completion of Alford No. 1. The field was named in honor of the Great Wildcatter by the Texas Railroad Commission.[205]

The Benedum Townsite, Block Y, Section 48, TC RR, and Block 4½, Section 10, GC & SF was dedicated by Mr. J. S. and Mrs. Arlisse Elliott and approved by the Upton County Commissioners' Court, November 14, 1949.

At the intersection of Highway 349 and FM Road 1555, an Official Texas State Marker was erected January 17, 1965, in Benedum's memory.

Active in his oil interests on his eighty-ninth birthday, he is reputed to have discovered more oil than any other person in history. He amased an oil fortune evaluated at more than eighty million dollars. He was one of the nation's wealthiest men and one of the largest taxpayers in America.

It was properly said of Benedum: "He has never bought a ticket on a horse race, tossed a chip on a roulette table, owned a share of stock, on margin, or even bet a nickel in penny ante poker, and denounced gambling to his associates. Yet, he is the greatest gambler in America, casually tossing as much as three million dollars into a wildcat prospect."[206]

Mr. Benedum passed away July 30, 1959.[207]

BONE, ERLE CARLE

Erle Carle Bone was born in Bryant, Indiana, October 17, 1894, the son of William J. and Polly Bone, and died in the Big Spring Veterans Hospital, May 23, 1960. He was buried in McCamey, Texas, May 24, 1960.

As it is the custom to hold Memorial Day Service at the grave of the last passing veteran, the service was held May 30, 1960, at the grave of Erle Bone, who, as Chaplain of the American Legion, planned the service before his death.[208]

Mr. Bone enlisted in World War I in 1917 and served in France and in Belgium until the end of the war. He was a member of *La Societe des 40 Hommes et 8 Chevaux* and was at the organizational meeting of the American Legion and remained a member until the time of his death. He was post commander of the American Legion Price Pool Post No. 421 in 1937 and was Chaplain at the time of his death. He became a member of the Veterans of Foreign Wars. For special trust and confidence in patriotism, valor and fidelity, he received citations from Governors W. Lee O'Daniel in 1941 and Coke Stevenson in 1943.

In 1930 he married Margaret Etta McCormick in San Antonio, Texas, then came to McCamey, where he engaged in the hardware business. He was instrumental in organizing the McCamey Chamber of Commerce. He served on the City Council from April 12, 1943, to November 8, 1948, when he became Mayor of McCamey and served for two years. He was an active worker in the First Presbyterian Church in McCamey and served as elder of the Church until his death.

Mr. Bone is survived by his wife and two daughters, Mrs. Curtis (Erlene) Thomas and Mrs. Jack (Mary Margaret) Milam, and one son, Captain James Arthur Bone, Operations Officer 728 Tactical Control Squadron Air Force.

CALDWELL, RUFUS ARTHUR II

Rufus Arthur Caldwell II was born June 9, 1902, son of Ruben Arthur and Mabelle (Molder) Caldwell in Corsicana, Texas.[209] He died after thirty-three years of service with the Humble Pipe Line Company in Big Lake, Texas, May 4, 1966, and at the time of his death was assigned to the Odessa District Office.[210] He came to Big Lake from McCamey in 1958 as Big Lake district clerk for Humble, West Texas Division, when district offices were established at Kemper Station. Fishing and baseball were his interests, and he played in the Texas League for a number of years. He continued the game in later years, coaching in Little League. He was active in McCamey Little League, and in Big Lake he helped Wilson Loftin with the winning Dodgers for two years.[211]

He was married to Roberta Sherrod, November 24, 1938, and they had two children, a son and a daughter. The daughter preceded him in death October 7, 1958. The family moved to McCamey in 1948. At the age of thirteen, his son, R. A. Caldwell III, joined Chapter 76, Junior Historians, giving his father another interest. Mr. Caldwell was a loyal though silent patron of the Mendoza Trail Museum. He, with his wife, gave their son support in Chapter activities. When the Plymouth Oil Company withdrew from Texon, Mr. and Mrs. Caldwell petitioned Mike Benedum for equipment for the Museum. Mr. Benedum authorized W. J. Grissett, in charge of the Plymouth Oil Company's facilities at Texon, to donate to the Mendoza Trail Museum, Inc., certain tools used by Plymouth in drilling early wells in the Plymouth — Big Lake — Texon Field including:

A 2755 Standard (Cable) Tool Bit Gauge
A 3⅞" Standard (Cable) Tool Bit Gauge
A hand operated Meyers low-down pump known by early oil field workers as a "One-Arm Johnny"
A tool for knocking water from the bit
A never-slip casing shoe
A jerk line saddle
A cabinet containing cores and isinglass

Mr. and Mrs. Caldwell were also hosts to Cecil Gill when he presented a contour map of Upton County on behalf of the Humble Pipe Line and the Humble Oil and Refining Companies.

DILLINGHAM, MAT

Mat Dillingham, son of William Brice and Sarah Margaret Dillingham, was born January 18, 1900, in Tye, Callahan County, Texas. He attended the Abilene public schools and was captain of his football team. He played football for two years at Abilene Christian College in the early twenties and transferred to Hardin-Simmons University when his coach transferred to that institution. Here he completed his football career. He was married to Miss Exie Jones in Stamford in March, 1924.

He joined the West Texas Utilities Company in June, 1925, in Abilene. He was transferred to Stamford as merchandise salesman. From here he was transferred in June of 1926 to Tuscola as local manager and then in the same capacity to Merkel. He was made group manager at Merkel in 1931. He then became assistant district manager in Abilene in July of 1937, and moved to McCamey in September, 1938, where he became assistant district manager.[212]

He was made District H Manager, June 15, 1943. He was faced with the problem of maintaining electric service to the vital oil industry during World War II. With critical shortages of wire, pole-line hardware, men and electrical apparatus, Mr. Dillingham and the other employees of the district maintained service to the oil fields and to the towns of the area.

Mr. Dillingham kept alive the company's tradition, a "Service Company," by taking his place as a civic leader in McCamey. His service activities include the directorship in the West Texas Chamber of Commerce, the District Chairman of the Permian Basin Boy Scout Area, receiving the top scouting award, The Silver Beaver, for his work with the boys of the area. He served as President of the Lions Club 1945-1946, having been a member since 1938.[213]

One of the greatest services he rendered was on the School Board of the McCamey Independent School Board when he was duly appointed to serve, April, 1941, and served until his death, February 6, 1950. He served as Finance Chairman, was elected Vice President of the Board, April 9, 1947, and as President on July 5, 1949. During his regime a new fence and lighting system were installed for the football field; streets were paved in front of the main school property on 11th Street, and on 6th and 7th Streets north and south of the Westover School, together with curb and gutter. Cold water drinking fountains were installed within the schools.[214]

Taking time out from his busy schedule, he often gave a hand during the shearing season at the John Cole Ranch. Then, with two or three companions, he would head for Lake Camargo, in Mexico. An expert at baiting the trot lines, he would capture a twenty-five or thirty-two pound cat or bass, much to the amazement of his companions.[215]

His untimely death February 6, 1950, left a void in the community and in the company which he served. The funeral services were held in the McCamey High School Auditorium at 10:00 A.M., February 8, 1950. A funeral cortege of more than twenty-five cars followed his remains to the Elmwood Memorial Park in Abilene, where graveside service was held at 4:00 P.M. He was survived by his widow; three sons, Mat Jr., Carrol Wayne and Lynn; and one daughter, Mrs. Saralu Brazell.

EARNEST, MRS. HENRY (EFFIE)

Mrs. Effie Earnest, born June 7, 1877, an orphan, married Henry Earnest, a cattle drover, in 1896 and came with him to Upton County that year. As a bride she arrived in the cow camp when she was nineteen years old.[216] She found life full of excitement, for a round-up was in full swing, and the cook had just left the country. Her first day in the county began at 4:00 A.M., when she started cooking breakfast for thirty-five men. The hard-riding cowhands required plenty of breakfast; so Mrs. Earnest served coffee, fried chicken, eggs, bacon, beef steak, sourdough biscuits, dried fruit, butter and gravy. As soon as the meal was over, she began the preparation of dinner, which was to be served at three in the afternoon. At sundown, supper had to be ready. That day left an indelible impression on her memory.[217]

Mrs. Earnest told me when I visited in her humble home facing the Upton County Courthouse, July 17, 1963, that her four-room house was moved to its present site in 1914. It had been placed on a "drag" in Upland, where it had been constructed in 1908, soon after Henry M. Halff had dedicated the townsite of Upland. After the dedication, Mr. Halff invited everyone present to go for a ride on the trail around the townsite. The ladies were seated inside his car, the children on the back and the men on the running board.

Many a day or night Mrs. Earnest would place her little children in the saddle with her and go to wait on sick men and women alike. Her skill and compassion were recognized by many.[218]

After round-ups were over, life became dull and drab in her little home, scantily furnished. It was lonely staying for six months in those early days without seeing the face of another woman, although men and cowboys would come by for food. She was never baffled by them, for she knew that cowboys, rustlers and even horse thieves had a profound respect for women. Actually, Mrs. Earnest could draw as fast a gun as the best of them. She was brave and absolutely fearless.

Mrs. Earnest lived through the good years and the bad years in Upton County for seventy years, a true pioneer. She died in St. John's Hospital, in San Angelo, Texas, after a long illness and was buried in the Rankin Cemetery, June 18, 1966. She is survived by one daughter, two grand-children and six great-grandchildren.[219]

ELLIOTT, DR. GEORGE WASHINGTON

Dr. George W. Elliott, son of Rueben and Elizabeth (Wilhite) Elliott, was born in Boone County, Kentucky, in 1830. He was educated for the practice of medicine. He married the former Miss Harriet McQuity in 1869 and moved to Bexar County, Texas, 1876.[220]

He had previously negotiated, May 6, 1876, for 1,700 acres of land for $3,454, a few miles northwest of San Antonio. He stocked his ranch with thoroughbred Durham cattle, using the brand "17." In 1884 he sold out to Thomas Pitt, realizing $18 an acre for his land and $100 a head for his stock.[221]

By 1884 Dr. Elliott had a 20,000 acre spread in Tom Green County along Mustang Creek, along Centralia Draw, along Wild China Pond Draw and the Horsehead Road.[222] He hauled water a distance of thirty miles by ox team to dig a well, getting water at a depth of thirty feet across from the Butterfield Stage Stand. He built a two-room rock house across from the stage stand. He placed 1,000 head of Stocker cattle on this range.

After the creation of Upton County, Dr. Elliott was appointed judge in 1889. Because of declining health, he sold his spread in 1890 and moved to Midland, Texas. He was elected chairman of the board for the organization of the First National Bank of Midland, Texas, in 1890.[223]

Dr. Elliott is credited with designing and patenting a saddlebag widely acclaimed by country physicians in the area.[224]

Dr. and Mrs. Elliott moved to Fort Worth, and he died there May 12, 1910. He is buried in the Oakwood Cemetery there.[225]

MR. AND MRS. JOHN WILLIS GARNER

John Willis Garner, son of Jesse Dan and Mattie Elizabeth Garner, was born July 16, 1876 in Lake Charles, Louisiana. His wife, Mamie Anolia Morrison, was born in Baylor County, Texas on March 29, 1884. They were married in Gilland, Texas, March 21, 1900.[226]

In 1902, Mr. Garner moved to Upton County where he worked for Clinton Giddings, a rancher. Garner and Giddings became partners and ranched near what later became Upland. This partnership was dissolved and Garner leased the ranch which was called "The Greasewood" and he branded his stock the greasewood.

Garner was active in organizing Upton County in 1910. He was elected and served as Commissioner of Precinct No. 2 in 1910-1911.

The ranch house where Mr. and Mrs. Garner lived served as the first court house in Upton County. Before a jail could be built, prisoners were chained to a tree at the Garner home, and meals for the prisoners were prepared by Mrs. Garner. After the rock court house was built with its jail, Garner purchased the old court house building and moved it to the ranch. It still stands today (1970) and is still occupied by the family, who ranch near where Upland used to be.

When the Kansas City, Mexico and Orient Railroad passed through Rankin, practically every family moved away from Upland, including the Garners. Mr. Garner, an active civic leader in the new town, helped build the Methodist Church. He was an active member of the A.F. & A.M. No. 1251 and was a Thirty-second Degree Mason; of the Independent Order of Odd Fellows No. 947; and of the Woodmen of the World. He was elected and served as sheriff and tax collector, 1917-1922 and also as commissioner of Precinct No. 1, 1927-1930.

Mr. Garner was a devoted husband and father. On one of his many trips to Kansas he often expressed concern as is evidenced by this letter:

Dearest Ones: Sept. 1918

Went out to ranch to-day, but cattle will land tomorrow, if I get cars will start home Sunday. Hope you got water starting out all OK by now. . . . Will be home just as soon as I can get loose here.

As ever yours,
J. W. Garner

Mr. and Mrs. Garner were the parents of eight children: Velma, J. D., Nora, Dollye, John W. Jr., Hattie, M. M., and Jack M.

John Willis Garner was well-known for his dry wit. On one occasion when asked if he was related to the former Vice President of the United States, John Nance Garner, he replied, "If he ever gets to be president, I'm going to try to claim kin."

After John Willis Garner passed his half century mark, he conceived the idea of having a horse ranch. He found a 100-section spread west of Girvin. He constructed a long adobe house and corrals for his head-quarters and stocked it with more than 1,000 head, some of the finest horses in Texas. When asked if he had raised horses all his life, he replied, "I haven't raised horses all my life. Just since I was about 15." [227]

Mr. Garner died on April 22, 1946. His wife died November 4, 1969.

HALAMICEK, EDWIN PETER

Edwin Peter Halamicek was born March 12, 1899, at Roznov, Texas. He was the son of John M. and Anna (Baron) Halamicek. He completed the eighth grade in the Roznov Schools, after which he attended the Sam Houston State Normal School. He attended The University of Texas and the Baylor Medical School, specializing in pharmacy. On June 9, 1923, he obtained his Certificate No. 6850 from the State Board.

Mr. Halamicek was employed as pharmacist in Bellville, Texas, until 1926, when he moved to McCamey and went to work as the first licensed pharmacist in Meyers Drug Store. In the fall of 1926 he was offered better opportunities in the Echo Drug Company, which he finally bought, and established one of the most modern drug stores in West Texas. Mr. Halamicek, a public spirited citizen, was a Charter Member of the McCamey Country Club, a member of the Masonic Lodge and the Odd Fellows Lodge, a director for many years of the Security State Bank and was a real estate developer. Always interested in progressive civic projects, Mr. Halamicek served on the city council from January 1, 1928, to April 5, 1932, and from April 7, 1937, to April 18, 1941. He served on the water board from October 2, 1942, to October 7, 1948.

Mr. Halamicek married Miss Lucille Fisher in Bellville, Texas, in 1925.

They had one son, Eddie P. Halamicek, who was an outstanding football player in high school. Football was a sport dear to Mr. Halamicek.

Mr. Halamicek, upon his return from a fishing trip to Port Isabel, was killed in an automobile accident, January 21, 1954. He was buried in the McCamey Cemetery January 23, 1954, with the pallbearers being the teammates of his son. Serving were Ronald Baron, Mickie Stephens, Paul Brown, Bobby Johnson, Jack Bryant, Charlie Dixon, all of McCamey, and Lynn Halamicek of Tahoka and Burwell Baron of Lubbock.[228]

HALFF, HENRY M.

Henry M. Halff, son of Mayer and Rachel Hart Halff, was born in San Antonio, Texas, August 17, 1874. He was educated in Stanton Military Academy, Virginia, and in Eastman Business College, Poughkeepsie, New York.[229]

On January 1, 1905, he married Miss Rosa Wechsler. Their children were Meyer H., Ernestine Julia (Mrs. Norman Freeman), Ray Elizabeth (Mrs. George Llewellyn), and Albert Halff.[230]

After their marriage, Mr. and Mrs. Halff moved to Midland, Texas, where they built a beautiful home, a center of culture and refinment.[231]

Mr. Halff inherited the vast estate in Midland, Upton, Crockett and Pecos Counties from his father. He engaged in the operation of the J. M., the Circle Dot and the Quien Sabe ranges of horses and cattle, and attempted to apply to his operations the most modern methods known at the time.[232]

Mr. Halff moved his ranch headquarters from Pontoon Crossing to the Elliott Rock House near Wild China Pond and across from the old Butterfield Stage Stand in Upton County. Dave Price was one of the drovers who moved the stock up the J. M. Draw (the Five Mile Creek). He stated that after having stopped at the new headquarters, when the separation of the stock was made, the cowboys continued with the herds to Midland to ship out. Eleven days were required to empty the shipping pens.[233]

Mr. Halff was a firm believer in breeding up his stock. He bred registered Hereford cattle and built show herds which captured ribbons in fairs at Fort Worth and Kansas City.[234]

He bought thoroughbred stallions from racing stables and bred them with local mares, producing a fast but wiry horse. He was ever on the alert for horses from ranches in the West. To show what these horses could do, he organized a polo team in Midland to compete with teams in that town. He took his teams on tours in the East. At Aikin, South Carolina; at Dedham, Massachusetts; and at Newport, Rhode Island,

Halff won trophies. He imported Belgian stallions which developed much more powerful draft horses.[235]

Henry M. Halff pioneered in the use of irrigation wells and showed what could be done with the land when it was irrigated. His grapes, pumpkins and fruit were a spectacular example of cultivation. An original well of his in the city of Midland is still in use.

Much of his spread was taken up by homesteaders when the Four-Section Land Bill was put into effect. He urged his cowboys to file on land in Upton County, promising to buy them out when they had complied with the law.

Mr. Halff, knowing the need for schools, dedicated the townsite Upland and sold lots for the price of a notary fee. He built a general merchandise house at Upland with a hotel on the second floor. He promoted the building of a schoolhouse. He established a reputation throughout West Texas of honesty and integrity toward all people.

The great drouth from 1914-1920 took its toll on this vibrant man. His declining health impelled him to move to Mineral Wells in 1924 and later to Dallas, and finally to Richardson, where he died in 1933 at the age of fifty-nine. He was buried in Emanuel Cemetery in Dallas, Texas.[236]

HALFF, MAYER

Mayer Halff was identified with the cattle industry of Texas and the western plains from the time of his arrival in Texas in 1850 until 1905, the time of his death. He was born in Lauterberg, France, and at the age of fourteen, he came to Galveston, Texas, to help his brother Adolphe, who was peddling merchandise from Galveston to Liberty on the Old Spanish Trail. Their business was so profitable that they opened a mercantile establishment in Liberty. Money was scarce, but cattle plentiful. Mayer accepted cattle for his merchandise and began trailing them to New Orleans over the Old Spanish Trail.[237]

Adolphe Halff sailed from Galveston, August 8, 1856, on the steamship *Nautilus* enroute to northern markets to purchase a stock of goods. A hurricane overtook the *Nautilus* and sank the ship with all on board.[238]

This left the twenty-year-old Mayer Halff with a tremendous burden. He wrote to a younger brother, Solomon, to come over and help. Solomon immediately set sail and arrived in Galveston, 1857. He was a proficient linguist, speaking English, French, German and Spanish. Not interested in cattle, he turned his efforts to the mercantile end of the business.

At the outbreak of the Civil War, Mayer was confronted with a dwindling market in New Orleans and also with a dwindling range for his fast-accumulating stock. In 1864 he and Solomon moved their business to San Antonio, and with a cousin of theirs, formed a wholesale dry goods company which operated under the firm name of Halff and Levy until 1868. The firm then took the name M. Halff and Brother.[239]

They acquired range land in the vicinity of Pena Colorada, Texas, stretching south of the town of Marathon. Their brand was the Circle Dot.[240]

This was only the beginning of their holdings in the Southwest. At the peak of their career, they controlled thousands of acres, either by purchase or by lease. In Crocket County they bought on the east side of the Pecos a fifty-mile stretch lying one section deep and leased thousands of acres adjoining their purchase. This was known as the J. M. Ranch.[241]

They headquartered at Pontoon Crossing and bought land on both sides of the J. M. Draw (Upton County) and acquired the Quien Sabe Ranch in Upton and Midland counties. Yet, these ranges were not the whole of the Halff holdings. They had ranches in Bee and McMullen Counties; the Mallett Ranch in Gaines County; they bought the Crouch Ranch in Frio County; and they were part owners of the Laramie Cattle Company in Wyoming, to which they would trail their cattle up from Texas to fatten for market.[242]

At the turn of the century Solomon Halff began selling out his interest in the cattle firm to Mayer Halff, who, in turn, listed his firm as Halff and Son.

Halff and Brother were among the first cattlemen to foresee the change in the cattle business. Long cattle drives were displaced by the coming of railroads. Cattle prices were declining. A better breed of cattle was in demand. The Legislature of the State of Texas was closing the open range and opening free grass to the homesteader. Mayer was seeking water. He drilled wells in Frio County, in Midland County and in Upton County. The parched land in Upton County failed to yield water. Time was running out on this great cattleman.

Mayer Halff never lost the adventuresome spirit on the cattle trail. He married Rachel Hart of Detroit, Michigan, and they made their home in San Antonio. To them were born four children, two daughters and two sons, Alex and Henry Mayer. Besides his abiding interest in the cattle industry, Mayer Halff helped found the City National Bank of San Antonio,[243] of which he was president until his death. He endeared himself to his employees, both on the range and in the bank. He was active in the affairs of Temple Beth-El, and at one time served as president of the Congregation. Mayer Halff was buried in Beth-El Cemetery in San Antonio.[244]

HARRIS, MRS. WALTER (MOTHER PERLE)

Mrs. Walter Harris, born in Byhalia (White Oak), Mississippi, August 30, 1872, was christened Perle Lyle. She was reared on the White Oak Plantation and educated in the Kate Tucker Institute.[245]

She married Walter Harris, a cotton planter, January 28, 1897. They had one son, Maburn Harris. When his wife died, leaving two little girls, the grandparents reared the girls. Mrs. Harris' high ideals and Christian teachings are reflected in the lives of her grandchildren, and, in the lives of the children of her neighborhood, by whom she was known as "Mother Perle." This spirited and cheerful person gave her time to others.[246]

Her going through a blinding snowstorm with her husband to Dawson County, Texas, in 1914, to open up a cotton industry in West Texas, is a testimony of this venerable lady's courage and fortitude. When their contract was fulfilled, she again pioneered with her husband to the oil boom town, McCamey, in 1927 to open up a grocery business. In 1930 they bought the Texas Hotel, and she operated it until 1952, nine years after the death of Mr. Harris in 1943.[247]

In civic affairs Mrs. Harris' responsibility was climaxed in 1948, when she was chosen "Sweetheart of McCamey." She was always willing to lend a helping hand regardless of race, color or creed.

Mother Perle was a charter member of All Saints Episcopal Church, the McCamey Parents-Teachers' Association, the McCamey Girl Scout Council and the McCamey Cemetery Association. She was responsible for obtaining the deed to the McCamey Cemetery and served as its publicity chairman for many years. She helped sponsor the Upton County Public Library, the Upton County Home Demonstration Club, the McCamey Garden Club and the McCamey Business and Professional Women's Club. She served as organizational chairman[248] of the McCamey Women's Study Club in 1929. Previously she had assisted in the organization of the Swan Lake, Mississippi, Women's Study Club and the organization of the Stonewall Jackson Daughters of the Confederacy, of which she was its State Recorder of Crosses in 1907. She organized the Daughters of the American Revolution in Tunica County, Mississippi in 1914. Mrs. Harris served as president of the Lamesa Study Club from 1925-1926.

In the McCamey Women's Study Club, Mrs. Harris served as federation councillor from 1929-1930; and from 1942-1943; from 1943-1944; and from 1944-1945. She served the Club as its program chairman, 1930-1931, and its membership chairman, 1932-1933.[249]

She maintained an active interest in its affairs, as well as a pertinent interest in local, state and national affairs until her final hospitalization. She died December 28, 1964, and is buried in the McCamey Cemetery.[250]

HIGDAY, MRS. E. C.

Mrs. E. C. Higday (Urbie Bessie Dilworth), born in Pleasanton, Texas, January 28, 1894, was the daughter of Mr. and Mrs. A. P. Dilworth. She moved with her family and settled on a farm in Buena Vista in 1912. Here the farm family struggled to eke out a living off cotton and grain. They attended the community church and the church-sponsored socials.

Urbie Bessie married E. C. Higday, June 22, 1913. For their honeymoon they proudly chose the ride from the newly built railroad station at Owego on the old Orient Railroad to Fort Stockton, where Mr. Higday took his bride to live. They moved to McCamey in 1927 and then on to Rankin in 1928. To this union were born three daughters, Joy, Mary and Marjorie.

In Rankin Mrs. Higday was an active member of the Methodist Church, a charter member of the Rankin Study Club, a charter member of the Upton County Historical Society, of which she served as president from 1964-1966, and a charter member of the Upton County Historical Survey Committee. Mrs. Higday was also a patron of the Midland High Sky Girls Ranch. The girls at the ranch attended her funeral en masse.

Mrs. Higday died December 31, 1967, and was buried in the Rankin Cemetery.

JOHNSON, THEODORE WILLIS

Theodore Willis Johnson, son of James Wesley and Annie (Houghton) Johnson, was born in Round Rock, Texas, August 15, 1893.[251] A month after his birth, he was brought to his home at Pontoon Crossing on the Pecos, where he stayed until he was old enough to go to school. He received his primary education in a covenant in San Angelo, Texas. At the age of fourteen he was entered in Dr. Moore's School in San Angelo.

He was engaged in the stock raising business — quarter horses, white-faced cattle, goats, sheep and bison.

Mr. Johnson married Alma Mae Matthews in Sonora, Texas, August 15, 1918. They ranched in Coke County and then moved to the Pecos, south of Sheffield. The ranch is still known as the Johnson Ranch.

Mr. and Mrs. Johnson were the parents of two sons and four daughters. They moved to Upton County in 1932 ten miles west of McCamey. He bought a ranch west of Deming, New Mexico, in 1948 and operated both ranches until his death, February 8, 1956.

Mr. Johnson was a widely and well-known rancher along the Pecos River. He was active in stock shows and in all phases of 4-H Club work, in which all of his children participated and carried off many first and second places. His son Tommy won first place in judging grasses and was awarded a trip to enter his exhibit in Chicago in 1946. The children at birth were given a herd of thoroughbred Herefords by their grand-father and the cattle bore the individual brands of each child.[252]

Mr. Johnson died February 8, 1956, and is buried in the Sheffield Cemetery.

LANE, MR. AND MRS. JOHN F.

John F. Lane and Almeda Graff East were married in the parsonage of Rev. Coon in San Angelo, Texas, on January 6, 1892.

Mr. Lane, whose parents were D. T. and Permelia (Clark) Lane, was born February 22, 1867, in San Saba County on the open range where the Indians were still troublesome. In 1881 the family moved to Lampasas County, where they established a ranch and engaged in freighting with oxen, as many as five yoke at a time. During the next few years John worked as a cowboy and a bronc buster in Fisher, Stonewall, Kent and Scurry Counties, where he was considered a top roper rider.

Miss Almeda East was born November 7, 1872, in Morgan County, Missouri. Her family moved to Burlington, Kansas, since her father was a section foreman for a railroad company, and two years later, moved to the Cherokee Strip in Indian Territory. Here the family was confronted with friendly Cherokee Indians. At the age of fourteen Allie moved with her family to Coffeeville, Kansas. The East children attended school wherever they lived. When Allie was sixteen the family moved to Lampasas, Texas. Three years later she married John F. Lane in San Angelo and returned with him in a covered wagon, the trip taking three days. They lived in Lampasas until 1895, when they moved to Coke County, entering the ranching business. In 1898 they moved to Scurry County, ranching on the side.

In 1904 Mr. and Mrs. Lane moved to Gaines County near Seminole, where they tried their hand at farming. The sand and the drouth were too much for them.

They turned to ranching again and moved to Upton County in 1907, making their last move in a covered wagon trailing their cattle behind them. They located their ranch east of King Mountain. This location proved fortunate for the Lanes. They began fencing it, for the land had the best winter pasturage in the country. Mr. Lane was active in organizing the county. Mrs. Lane was determined that her children should have an education. She took them to Stiles (Reagan County), thirty-five miles away, during the school term until the Rankin school was established, which the Lanes helped build.[253]

A citizen of Upton County, Mr. Lane in 1910 petitioned the State Legislature for the organization of Upton County with Upland as the county seat. He was elected one of the commissioners of the commissioners' Court. He served eight years.[254]

According to an account of his grandson, a neighbor of Lane's, a Mr.

Smith who owned half interest in a ranch with Lane, said he would give half interest in the half he owned if someone would put water on it. John F. Lane drilled a well on this land and got half interest on it. Then, a few years later, Mr. Smith sold the other half to Mr. Lane.[255]

In June, 1925, George B. McCamey drove his car up to the porch of John F. Lane, who had been recommended to McCamey as the most knowledgeable man regarding a site in Upton County on which to drill a wildcat well. A fast friendship grew up between the wildcatter and the rancher.

Lane furnished his teams for digging the slush pit for the wildcatter's well. When the well came in, McCamey drilled in the second well in the McCamey Field for the rancher.[256]

Except for the original Yates Ranch Gusher of 1926, Weir No. 1 Oil Well in Upton County is the most dramatic oil discovery (1961). This is the "first quadruple completion in West Texas, called by the American Association of Petroleum Engineers the most important development of the year 1961 and the most prolific discovery in many years."[257] This well is one of the many wells drilled on the John F. Lane Ranch in Upton County.

On July 1, 1927, when the First State Bank was opened in Rankin, Lane was chosen president and served in that capacity until 1928.[258]

Mr. and Mrs. Lane had lived in Lampasas, Coke, Gaines, Scurry and Pecos counties. In Upton County they had owned in fee or leased 105 sections of land and ran some 2,000 head of cattle.

By 1936 the Lanes bought a ranch in Brewster County and made their last move, but not in a covered wagon trailing their cattle behind them. Everything was moved in a large trailer truck. This was the place Mrs. Lane liked best of all, where they had their beautiful ranch home and where Mrs. Lane grew impatient when they heard of the "Good Old Days."

Mr. Lane passed away April 3, 1958, survived by Mrs. Lane until March 26, 1965.

LITTLEJOHN, MARGARET E. (MRS. W.W.)

Margaret Etta, born to a school teacher and his wife, Mr. and Mrs. Hicklyn, in a wagon train just outside Prescott, Arizona, on December 15, 1882, lived an eventful life for seventy-nine years.

As a child, she lived during Indian raids in Arizona and New Mexico. As a fifteen year old bride, she went with her husband, Henry Davidson, a mining engineer, to visit his family in England. They then went to Guanajuato, Mexico, where her husband was the manager of a silver mine. To this union were born three sons, Henry, Oscar and Tommy. Her husband died, leaving her a widow in Guanajuato. After two years, she married Robert McCormack from Edinburg, Scotland, manager of British interests in Guanajuato. He later became a British consul. To this union were born Margaret (Mrs. E. C. Bone of McCamey) and Josephine (Mrs. R. W. White of San Antonio). When the Mexican Revolution broke out, the McCormacks were in a party of six families who fled Mexico and Pancho Villa's regime.[259] They rode a military freight train draped with a British flag. The families were hundled in one end of the box car, with kegs of dynamite in the other end. After he established his family in El Paso, Mr. McCormack returned to Mexico to look after business interests. There he died and was buried in Mexico City, 1917.[260]

Next Margaret Etta married her third husband, W. W. Littlejohn, a consignee of Gulf Oil Company in El Paso, Texas. In 1927 the company transferred Mr. Littlejohn to McCamey, Texas. Mr. and Mrs. Littlejohn took up their residence in a tent north of the Orient Railroad tracks until they could build a house. Mrs. Littlejohn recalled those days as being "dust fender high," filling the air. She did something about this. She fenced her yard and brought in redbud trees and other plants from the canyons in the nearby mesas. She had a water system installed and a small pool constructed. Her wide porch facing the south was decorated with Mexican pottery, fabrics and sombreros. She opened a Mexican kitchen, which was welcomed by men and women.

She was a collector of rocks and shells and with a companion would go into the hills to bring them back. It is no wonder that in her quieter moments she would paint in oil. She was artistic in matching colored fabrics for quilts and rugs. Her children, grandchildren and great grand-children treasure the keepsakes she left them.

Four of her grandchildren took an active part in Chapter 76 of the McCamey Junior Historians. Elizabeth and Mary Etta Littlejohn constructed figures for dioramas; Gary Oscar Davidson took seven trips to Old Fort Davis and constructed a diorama of that old fort; Jimmy Bone served the chapter three different years as president.

Mrs. Littlejohn was keenly interested in all their activities. She generously encouraged them and gave to the Mendoza Trail Museum many items of historic interest. She died in the Eden Nursing Home, May 29, 1963, and is buried in the McCamey Cemetery.[261]

MCCAMEY, GEORGE B.

George B. McCamey, son of Samuel Rogers and Frances (McKnall) McCamey, was born in Ridgeway, Elk County, Pennsylvania, November 11, 1882. When he was five years of age, the family moved to Davis, West Virginia, where George received his formal education. At the age of fifteen he left school, much too early, according to his father. The urge for new worlds to conquer became too strong to resist.[262]

His first work in the oil field was at Murphytown, West Virginia, for the South Penn Oil Company, when he assisted his uncle in cleaning out old oil wells. Following this experience came the desire to go to West. Money being scarce, he started for Beaumont, Texas via many jobs en route in one oil field or another. In Independence, Kansas, he worked on a lease as a roustabout, but in a short time he became a tool dresser. At Bridgeport, Illinois, he owned and operated his first "string of tools" (cable tool rig). Next he went to the Indian Territory, to Louisiana, and then wildcatting in Utah, South Dakota, Wisconsin and Montana before his return to Oklahoma in 1911, which now had been a state for four years.[263]

While in Oklahoma, he met and married Miss Olive Lankford of Beggs, Okmulgee County, January 13, 1916. There were four children: three daughters Virginia (Mrs. John A. Merrit), Georgia (Mrs. Henry T. Fair, Jr.) and Jacquelyn (Mrs. F. Hilton Lacy, Jr.), and a son, Robert L., born September 27, 1925, the same day the McCamey Discovery Well came in.[264]

George McCamey arrived in Texas to stay after operating out of Eldorado, Kansas, followed by eighteen months in Kentucky. In Fort Worth he established a home and maintained an office for forty years.

With several strings of tools, Mr. McCamey came into that part of Texas known geologically as the Permian Basin. His brother, Ray E. McCamey, was his general superintendent of field activity. Operations were carried on in Sweetwater, Bronte, Big Lake, Texon and Best, in both proven and unproven country.[265]

Having a keen interest in drilling wildcat country, he was approached and was offered 4,000 acres in Upton County if he would drill a test well. He accepted this offer with a partner, J. P. Johnson, a Fort Worth oil operator. Together they drilled the No. 1 M. L. Baker, SE¼ of the NE¼ Section 8, G.C. & S.F. Ry. Survey, which opened the McCamey Field in Upton County and ultimately created the town of McCamey.

Upton County, a rough terrain of approximately 1,300 square miles, had Rankin, the county seat and the only town in the county. There were only dirt roads in 1925, little more than trails crisscrossing the sprawling arid ranch lands covered with desert growth. There was little change since the days of covered wagon trains passing through to the West. But not for long. Roads were vital to this new undertaking. Everyone gave his time and energy to blaze the trail to the new (well) location. George often recalled in conversation with his friends: "It was pretty rough country in this area at that time, and I had some misgivings as to the drilling of the well. I remember the difficulty I had before the

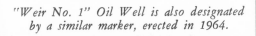

THE BENEDUM OIL FIELD AND
BENEDUM TOWNSITE
(ABOUT 4 MI. EAST)

FIELD NAMED IN 1950 BY TEXAS RAILROAD COMMISSION
IN HONOR OF MICHAEL LATE (MIKE) BENEDUM, 1869-1959,
WHO DEVOTED 69 OF HIS 90 YEARS TO THE OIL BUSINESS,
AND WON FORTUNE AND FAME AS "THE GREAT WILDCATTER".

HIS WORK BEGAN IN 1890, WITH A PARTNER, JOE C. TREES,
HE DISCOVERED OR DEVELOPED OIL FIELDS IN ILLINOIS,
WEST VIRGINIA, LOUISIANA (THE GREAT CADDO FIELD), THE
TUXPAM IN MEXICO, DEMARES IN COLOMBIA, SOUTH AMERICA,
AND IN TEXAS THE DESDEMONA, BIG LAKE, YATES, EAST
WHITE POINT, SUSAN PEAK AND BENAVIDES.

DISCOVERY OF BIG LAKE FIELD (1923) ON UNIVERSITY OF
TEXAS LAND TAPPED THE GREAT WEALTH OF THE PERMIAN
BASIN, WHICH OPENED IN 1920 WITH A SMALL DISCOVERY.
ALFORD NO.1, ORIGINAL WELL IN BENEDUM FIELD (LATER
RECLASSIFIED AS A GAS FIELD), WAS COMPLETED JAN. 4,
1948, AT DEPTH OF 12,011 FEET BY SLICK-URSCHEL OIL
CO., UNDER A PARTNERSHIP AGREEMENT. THE FIELD LATER
BENEFITED BY DEDICATION OF BENEDUM TOWNSITE.

THE "GREAT WILDCATTER" WAS AN OIL PIONEER WHOSE
WORK ENRICHED ONE OF THE WORLD'S LARGE CONSTITU-
TIONAL PERMANENT UNIVERSITY FUNDS. REVENUES FROM
OIL AND GAS OPERATIONS GIVE TEXAS THE LARGEST
PERMANENT PUBLIC SCHOOL FUND IN THE WORLD.
(1965)

*The Benedum Oil Field and Benedum Town-
site is identified by this roadside marker,
erected in 1965 by the Texas State Historical
Survey Committee.*

*"Weir No. 1" Oil Well is also designated
by a similar marker, erected in 1964.*

"WEIR NO. 1" OIL WELL

EXCEPT FOR THE ORIGINAL YATES RANCH GUSHER OF 1926,
MOST DRAMATIC OIL DISCOVERY IN UPTON COUNTY BROUGHT
IN DECEMBER 6, 1961, WEST OF THIS SITE 3.5 MILES.

FIRST QUADRUPLE COMPLETION IN WEST TEXAS, CALLED
BY AMERICAN ASSOCIATION OF PETROLEUM ENGINEERS THE
MOST IMPORTANT DEVELOPMENT OF THE YEAR 1961 — AND
THE MOST PROLIFIC DISCOVERY IN MANY YEARS. DRILLED
TO DEPTH OF 12,432 FEET, PLUGGED BACK AT 9,925 FEET.
PRODUCES FROM UPPER, MIDDLE AND LOWER STRAWN ZONES,
AND FROM THE BEND WITH PERFORATIONS IN LOWER DETRI-
TAL GAS ZONE. CONTRACTOR WAS BRAHANEY DRILLING CO.

DISCOVERY MADE BY E. G. RODMAN, W. D. NOEL AND ODESSA
NATURAL GASOLINE CO., FOUNDED BY RODMAN AND NOEL AND
AFFILIATED WITH EL PASO NATURAL GAS PRODUCTS CO.

RODMAN AND NOEL, WHO BEGAN THEIR UPTON COUNTY OPER-
ATIONS IN 1940, HAVE BEEN RESPONSIBLE FOR NUMEROUS
SIGNIFICANT DISCOVERIES IN THE PERMIAN BASIN OF
TEXAS AND NEW MEXICO, AND HAVE LED IN THE ESTABLISH-
MENT OF A VAST PETROCHEMICAL COMPLEX IN ODESSA. THIS
UTILIZES IN THE MAKING OF SUCH THINGS AS PLASTICS,
MANY PETROLEUM BY-PRODUCTS ONCE SCRAPPED AS WASTE.

SUCH LEADERSHIP AND SUCH WELLS AS WEIR NO.1 HAVE
ENABLED UPTON COUNTY TO REMAIN FOR MANY YEARS ONE
OF THE OUTSTANDING PRODUCTION AREAS IN TEXAS.
(1964)

RODMAN-NOEL OIL FIELD

DISCOVERED 1953. INITIAL WELL, ABOUT 2½ MILES
SOUTH OF THIS SPOT, WAS DRILLED BY E. G. RODMAN AND
W. D. NOEL AS NO. 1 RADFORD GROCERY. IT WAS COMPLETED
JANUARY 13, 1953, FOR A NATURAL FLOWING POTENTIAL OF
960 BARRELS IN 24 HOURS, FROM GRAYBURG FORMATION
AND AT TOTAL DEPTH OF 1744 FEET. IT IS LOCATED 1980
FEET FROM THE SOUTH AND WEST LINES OF SECTION 1 OF
THE GULF, COLORADO AND SANTA FE SURVEY IN RAILROAD
COMMISSION DISTRICT 7C.

THE FIELD HAS A NUMBER OF WELLS COMPLETED FOR
NATURAL POTENTIALS IN EXCESS OF 3,000 BARRELS A DAY.

THE DRILLERS RODMAN AND NOEL WERE OIL BUSINESS
VETERANS AT THE TIME THEY BROUGHT IN THIS UPTON
COUNTY FIELD, ALREADY EXPERIENCED IN VARIOUS PHASES
OF PETROLEUM DEVELOPMENT. E. G. RODMAN BECAME AN
INDEPENDENT PRODUCER IN TEXAS IN 1938. W. D. NOEL
BECAME AN INDEPENDENT PRODUCER IN TEXAS IN 1940.
THEIR INTERESTS EXTEND INTO INTERNATIONAL EXPLORA-
TION AND OTHER PHASES OF OIL DEVELOPMENT INCLUDING
MANUFACTURE OF PETROCHEMICALS.

THEIR OPENING OF THIS FIELD -- WHICH CONTRIBUTED
SUBSTANTIALLY TO THE 1925-60 UPTON COUNTY TOTAL OF
272,628,476 BARRELS OF PRODUCTION -- WAS MADE 28
YEARS LATER THAN THE GREAT BOOM IN McCAMEY.
(1964)

*Rodman-Noel Oil Field, discovered in 1953,
is identified by a marker erected in 1964.*

The Wilshire Plant (above) and Pembrook Plant (below) of the El Paso Natural Gas Company, both located in Upton County.

The McCamey Tank Farm (above) and Mesa Station (below) operated by Shell Oil Company to stock refineries in the Houston area.

The John W. Garner Family in a 1942 photo, included J. W. Garner and Mrs. Mamie Garner holding the baby, Jack M. Garner. Also in the group are Velma, Jesse Dan, Nora, Dollye, John Willie, Jr., Hattie, and M. M. "Bud" Garner.

John W. Garner proudly displays one of his horses in this 1942 photo.

material was moved in for this well in locating the spot where the location was staked, and truthfully, I do not think I would ever have found the stake, but for the help of Mr. John Lane, who had helped with the survey work."

Few residents other than the ranchers in that particular area could have known the location of the tract upon which the well was to be drilled. Mr. Lane owned a ranch situated between Rankin and the present town of McCamey. He had been recommended to Mr. Mc-Camey as being the one person who could assist in finding the beginning points in order that the surveyor could make the location on the right tract of land.

Another incident pointing up the stable relationship, the depth of friendship that existed between these two friends, their unquestionable faith in the integrity of one for the other was: George bought fifty or sixty head of Hereford cattle from Lane, leaving the selection entirely up to Lane. Upon the arrival of the cattle and after looking them over, McCamey made the comment, "These are better cattle that Old John selected than I would have received had I sent someone out to select them for me."

Many times when the rains came, the hurriedly built roads leading to well locations became almost impassable for any kind of transportation. Moving heavy equipment presented many problems. The location for Baker No. 1 was four miles north of the Orient Railroad. It would be a great convenience if a siding could be built on which material might be shipped by rail and switched on to the siding to await the unloading. With this thought in mind, Mr. McCamey approached Mr. Clary of the Orient. It was agreed that the Orient would furnish the necessary materials and supervision, with McCamey providing the labor. Whereupon, Clary added, "If you bring in a well, I will have a boxcar moved in by the switch with 'McCamey' emblazoned on it in white." True to his promise, this was done, and the town McCamey came into being.[266]

In September, 1926, one year after the discovery well, Mr. McCamey fulfilled a dream he had always held — that of organizing an oil company. He merged with the Union Land Company, an English organization which owned approximately 100,000 acres of Texas land in fee in Presidio, Pecos, Crane, Ector, Crockett and Upton counties, with offices in New York. The Cordova Union Oil Corporation was the result. Herbert Noble, a New York attorney and a stockholder in the English land company, was elected president of the Cordova Union Oil Corporation, maintaining general offices in New York City. Mr. McCamey was elected vice president and general manager of operations, with offices in Fort Worth, Texas. Then, McCamey was elected president of the corporation after the death of Noble in 1934 and served in this capacity until June, 1943, when Cordova Union was sold to the Atlantic Refining Company, now Atlantic Richfield Company.[267]

The Cordova Union, under the able management of Mr. McCamey, had developed an exceptionally strong position among the larger producing units of the oil industry in Texas and held a position of leadership in various sections of Texas for a number of years.[268]

Mr. McCamey continued his interest in the oil business as an independent producer and remained actively identified with the drilling and productive branch of the industry throughout his life.

He was held in high esteem by the oil fraternity, and he valued highly the close friendships formed at home and throughout the states in which he operated.

Through the years Mr. McCamey was associated with civic, social and business organizations, earning the friendship and good will of his fellow citizens.

When asked about his hobbies, his reply was, "My business is my hobby." He enjoyed every phase of the oil business, coming up through the ranks from roustabout to president of a successful oil company. This was his hobby until 1934. In that year he began his first real hobby, a stock farm for raising thoroughbred horses.

He purchased 550 acres of land in Bedford, Tarrant County, twenty miles northeast of Fort Worth and ten miles north of the W. T. Waggoner Race Track, Arlington Downs, at Arlington. In a heavily wooded 160 acre tract he had three large barns built with paddocks and arranged for the small fields adjacent to be used for brood mares and their foals. Near the entrance to the farm, a half mile track was built with a cooling barn of eleven stalls, feed and tack rooms and quarters for grooms. Horses in training at the farm were kept at the barn. This was Mr. McCamey's pride and pleasure.

Two of the first horses to win races for his Bedford Stock Farm were Dedication and Centennial. Two of McCamey's better known stake horses were Royal Countess and Robert L., the latter named for Mr. McCamey's only son. Robert L. raced with many wins to his credit at Arlington as did Royal Countess. Both horses went on to win at Santa Anita (California), Hileah (Florida), Jamaica (New York), Washington Park (Chicago) and Churchill Downs (Louisville). Horses carrying the green and white silks of his stock farm raced across the nation and also in Mexico City. Mr. McCamey shipped his stable in April, 1945 to Mexico City to race at the Hipodromo de Las Americas, selling his horses and equipment before the meet was over. Mr. McCamey was an active member of the Thoroughbred Horse Association of Texas, serving as vice president in 1936.[269]

Although he never lived in the town that bore his name, he always maintained interests in its growth and development. His benefactions were numerous. When the Girl Scouts organization was being formed in McCamey in 1939, and when Mr. McCamey was advised of the great need for funds, he generously gave a sizeable amount to the organization. He likewise gave liberal support to religious and civic organizations in the town.

The town of McCamey looked forward with a great deal of pride in having him, his wife and son as their honored guests. He took great pride in attending town celebrations and making new friends and renewing old friendships. It was during the 35th Anniversary Celebration that Mr. McCamey passed away after several years of illness. Honoring his memory a memorial service was held at the site of the Discovery Well on June 22, 1960, while simultaneously his funeral services were held in the University Christian Church at Fort Worth.

M^CELROY, JOHN T.

John T. McElroy, born in Ohio, 1849, and reared in Iowa, came to Texas in 1873, where he established a ranch in Dimmit County. Two years later he came to Reeves County, establishing his headquarters in Pecos City.[270]

According to Paul Patterson of Crane, Texas, Mr. McElroy took 2,000 head of cattle from Guaymas, Mexico, and trailed them three years to Kansas via Nacogdoches and Horsehead Crossing.[271]

In 1875 he ran his cattle on the open range in Reeves, Loving and Pecos counties. He went up the trail in 1886 and for the following twenty-four years. He married Miss Mamie Parker in Pecos City. She survived Mr. McElroy, who died in Hotel Dieu, El Paso, October 13, 1936.[272]

McElroy bought the Jigger Y Ranch in 1894 from Union Beef Company of Chicago, claiming forty miles of land on both sides of the Pecos River from Toyah to the eastward.[273]

In 1897 the Western Union Beef Company, ranging on both sides of the Pecos from Toyah to its mouth, began selling its land and cattle. That year the "7D" brand and four hundred sections of land were sold to John T. McElroy of Pecos.[274]

These sections lay within Pecos, Crane and Upton Counties. Mr. McElroy took possession of 10,000 cattle from the 7D's a unit of Western Union Beef, at Horsehead Crossing and Castle Gap.[275]

The cluster of buildings at the McElroy headquarters in Upton County are neat and well-kept. They include an office, two family houses, a bunk house for cowboys and a commissary from which all hands may draw their supplies.[276]

Near the head of a draw coming off King Mountain where Mr. McElroy had established his headquarters, he and his wife frequently came

out on tours of inspection. He had an agreement with Carl Aiken of
Odessa, who had a Model T Ford, that any time, day or night, that
McElroy and/or his wife got off the train, Mr. Aiken would take them
to the ranch, some thirty-six miles. The round trip was all day or all
night, and the fee was $10.00.[277]

On June 28, 1907, with T. H. Bauchamp, Mr. McElroy established the
First National Bank in Pecos, of which he remained president until his
death.[278]

McElroy organized the El Paso Packing Company in 1921. This company was recognized as one of the finest packing companies in the
section.[279]

Many of the homesteaders who had taken up their four sections of
land from 1895 to 1910 were being wiped out by the drouth. McElroy
began buying them out.[280]

It seemed that Mr. McElroy had about everything — range, cattle, a
packing plant and a bank. But still a greater fortune was thrust upon
him. Oil was discovered in the Church and Fields Well several miles
from the land that McElroy owned. He had leased his entire ranch for
oil and gas. O. C. Harper was zone geologist for Gulf and leased 18,000
acres for his company, which brought in the discovery well, the J. T.
McElroy No. 1, June 1, 1926.[281]

Mr. McElroy was not interested in oil or oil men. He closed his
negotiations with a Frenchman, De Caplane, who was the principal
owner of the Franco-Wyoming Oil Company and also the president of
a bank in Paris, France. The deal was closed March 3, 1927, for
$2,500,000, including 68,720 acres with mineral interests and not less
than 6,000 cattle and all horses and mules. This spread lay in Crane,
Pecos and Upton Counties.[282]

John T. McElroy is buried in the family plot in Pecos, Texas.

MATEJOWSKY, EMMET

Emmet Matejowsky, the son of Mr. and Mrs. Anton Matejowsky, was
born in Dime Box, Texas, November 3, 1902, and died in McCamey,
Texas, October 15, 1965. He attended the Oklahoma Agricultural College in 1923-1924 and in 1924-1925. He transferred to The University
of Texas in the fall of 1925.[283]

In the summer of 1926, he was commissioned by W. A. Halamicek to
manage a newly constructed grocery and general merchandise store on
Fifth Street in McCamey, then a boom town in the Permian Basin.
Halamicek sold to Matejowsky the grocery department of this store
in 1933.[284]

During the depression years, 1932-1939, Mr. Matejowsky was able to
keep the doors of his store open and became a well-known business man

in the area. He moved his place of business across the street and changed the name to Matejowsky Food Center.

On December 1, 1948, Mr. C. W. Brown leased to Mr. Matejowsky a beautiful modernly equipped glass-front facility for a grocery store. Today, twenty-one years later, at 224 East Sixth Street, 1900 square feet have been added to the original 5606 square feet, in which are housed a food department, a meat market, drug supplies and household wares. The building has a refrigerated air system to welcome the patronage. The store bears the title Matejowsky's Food Center, a fitting legacy for the man who sank his roots in the once boom town, stayed through the Depression, and helped to build a better town.

Mr. Matejowsky served on the City Council from April 12, 1943, to April 7, 1953. He also served on the Upton County (McCamey) Park Board from 1939-1943. He married Miss Elizabeth Ann Baron, March 31, 1928. To this union were born two children, Frederick, and Mrs. Dale (Betty Jo) Kluthe. They have three grandchildren who are carrying on the ideals and aspirations of their grandparents.

PATTERSON, JUDGE JOHN D.

John D. Patterson, son of William T. and Mary (Earnest) Patterson, was born February 18, 1869, in Fannin County, Texas. The family, passing "through Dallas, Texas, was offered a quarter of section of land for their splendid yoke of oxen and a new wagon, but they preferred moving farther west."[285]

From Hood County they moved near a little community, Pontotoc. Patterson's father was a freighter and farmer, and he tells of his mother cooking cornbread, meat, mustard greens and wild onions, various wild fruits and berries on the open fire. Wild cattle roamed the brush— cattle that had no brand. These mavericks were a source of meat, if ammunition could be obtained.

The Patterson family moved out to Mitchell County, where John D. went to work for Col. C. C. Slaughter freighting supplies for the Colonel's widely scattered ranches. He finally got a job as cowboy with the Colonel.

Mr. Patterson remembered a torrential rain that started on the morning of July 18, 1893. He figured from the depth of the water in a doorless iron safe lying with its face up that the rain (which lasted two days and nights) must have been between 15" and 18".[286]

After 1900 for a dozen years he worked on various ranches in Gaines, Yoakum, Sterling, Howard and Reagan Counties. In Reagan County he served as Cattle Inspector from 1911-1913. In 1913 he worked for the Harris Brothers Ranch west of Rankin in the J. M. Draw (Upton County).

Mr. Patterson moved to the old town of Upland where he freighted, built fences, windmilled, carpentered and did occasional ranch work. While in Upland, he also served as County Treasurer and worked in the office of Sheriff John Garner.

In 1900, Mr. Pattarson married Miss Eula Pollard. To them were born seven children.

During the drouth, 1913-1920, Mr. Patterson took his sons to work in the hay fields of Balmorhea and the Mills' farm near Fort Stockton. One of his sons worked on the McElroy Ranch, while the other was engaged as a merchant on the same ranch.

Then back to Rankin he went, where he was engaged in taking down telephone lines from old Upland to Rankin. He continued freighting, fencing and carpentering. In 1923 he was appointed by the Commissioners' Court to fill the unexpired term of Judge J. H. Felps at $600.00 per year. To make ends meet, he continued freighting — this time by motor truck — gasoline, stock feed to various ranches and posts and wire for fences. He hauled wool and mohair back to Rankin. He resigned from the Judge's office in 1928 at the age of 59.

Mr. Patterson bought a small farm in the Checkerville Community, near Mineral Wells. At the age of 79 he sold his farm and bought a place in town with a "patch of land" big enough for a good sized garden, which he continued to work until his 96th year. After that, he limited his activities to walking and a little yard work.[287]

Judge Patterson died October 17, 1966, as a result of a fall, spending only two hours in a hospital out of his 97 years. He is survived by his second wife, the former Mrs. Sadie Carter, and three sons and three daughters.[288]

PITTMAN, M. E.

M. E. Pittman, the son of Howell Cobb and Mary (Rogers) Pittman, was born in Nicholson, Georgia, November 28, 1876. While still a small boy, he moved with his parents to Carthage, Texas. His first job was working in the newspaper office of the Carthage *Banner* as a printer's "devil." In 1881, he started working at his father's sawmill, and, while still in high school, he became a member of a construction crew.[289]

In 1899 he entered the light and power industry, installing the Carthage Plant, serving as the superintendent of this plant until 1911, when he went to Center, Texas, assuming duties as superintendent of the Center Ice, Light and Power Company until 1915, from which time he served as division superintendent of the Texas Gas and Electric Company in Center. He went to Amarillo in 1917 and became service manager of the Western Motor Company. He became assistant manager for the Utility Properties in Cisco, February 1, 1925, when he began his long and useful career with Texas Utilities Company.[290]

Mr. Pittman started his duties in the McCamey area, August 5, 1927, as District Manager, planning and building ahead for the future growth of the Permian Basin Oil Fields. On that date West Texas Utilities Company served only five wells — 18 months later W.T.U. served 14 pipeline stations; 40 wells were being pumped with electricity in the McCamey, Yates and Powell Fields.

In 1928 the Company had 11 miles of 11,000 volt line in the Powell Field; 55 miles of 11,000 volt line in the McCamey Field; and 40 miles of 11,000 volt line in the Yates Field.[291]

He established a routine of working 18 or 19 hours a day. Retiring at 2:00 A.M. and up at 7:00 o'clock A.M., he set the pace for the entire district operations. He brought electric power to the Permian Basin and also service to the area in which he lived. He joined in every civic activity, helping to build a city out of an oil boom town. He was a Mason, a member of the Lions Club and a member of the Christian Church. He spent 18 of his 44 years in the industry, retiring from the McCamey office in June of 1943. He died in San Angelo, August 23, 1950, and was buried in Fairmount Cemetery in San Angelo on August 25, 1950. Survivors are his widow, Whitney Pittman; one son, M. H. Pittman; and one daughter, Mrs. J. Paul Green.

POWERS, DR. HOMER

Dr. Homer Powers, born in 1856, at Point Pleasant, Virginia, son of Mr. and Mrs. Powers, at the age of 14 years, told his mother that he was going to Texas to become a cowboy, whereupon, she replied, "Settle down, young man; you are going to get an education, and be a man among men." He remained at home in Point Pleasant and prepared for medical school. He went to the College of American Medicine in St. Louis, where he obtained his medical degree in 1877.[292]

Before Powers fulfilled his boyhood dreams of "going to Texas," he practiced medicine for a short time in Illinois, where he became especially well known in treating pneumonia. Dr. Powers moved to Pecos City in Reeves County, Texas, where he visited the sick on widely scattered ranches.

In 1890 Dr. Powers moved to Fort Stockton where, in addition to maintaining his medical practices, he served actively in civic affairs. He was elected County Judge in 1906 and served until 1910. During this term the Commissioners' Court called for an election for a $15,000.00 bond for a school building. He initiated the survey of a road to Salt Crossing on the Pecos River; he granted a telephone franchise in May, 1909; and an electric light franchise in 1910.[293]

Late in the fall of 1915, Dr. Powers was called to the quicksilver mining communities of Terlingua and Boquillas to treat the sick. Soon after his arrival at Boquillas, a group of Pancho Villa's men raided the town and took several captives, including Dr. Powers. Dr. Powers helped the prisoners escape and guided them back to Texas and Alpine.[294]

In the year following the Boquillas Episode, Dr. Powers moved from Fort Stockton to Rankin, Texas, in Upton County, where there was a great need for a physician. Here, Dr. Powers continued his career as a physician and a public servant. He served as Tax Assessor from 1920-1924,[295] and as a school board member and as County Health Officer from 1916-1935.

As the first County Health Officer, Powers insisted on the immunization of school children against smallpox and typhoid fever. With the help of the school teachers, he held his clinic in the school building. As a member of the school board, he was instrumental in raising teachers' salaries and in appropriating money for reference facilities in the school library. He was also interested in wider knowledge of the Spanish language, organizing two classes under the guidance of the Extension Division of The University of Texas.[296]

Dr. Powers attended regularly throughout his career the State Medical Association and the Texas Railways Surgeons Meetings. He had a high regard for his colleagues in the medical fraternity, who often referred to him as an "old country doctor who was more modern that most of the younger doctors."[297]

When oil was discovered in Upton County in 1925, the population increased from 300 to 5,000 almost overnight. The demand for medical services accordingly increased, and Dr. Powers built the first hospital in McCamey. In a short time, according to the records of druggists, fifteen doctors were having prescriptions filled. The newcomers were received by Dr. Powers with professional courtesy.

Untiring in his efforts to serve his community, Dr. Powers often said he wanted to die in the harness. His wish was granted, for he continued to serve as Health Officer of Upton County until his death on June 28, 1935, in a San Angelo Hospital[298]

RANKIN, FINIS EWING AND ELIZA (SMITH)

Finis Ewing Rankin was born January 27, 1856, in Bedford County, Tennessee, the son of Robert Donnell and Matilda (Lynch) Rankin. His wife, Eliza's, maiden name Smith is most difficult to trace.[299] To Mr. and Mrs. F. E. Rankin were born three children, a daughter Maude, and two sons, Jesse Pearl and Robert Porter, all born in Bedford County, Tennessee..

Finis Ewing Rankin, having been told by his nephew (a school teacher in Midland, Texas) in 1896, of a "virgin" land of great range grass, abundance of water, herds of antelope and a variety of wild game, rugged men building ranches and gathering cattle, sensed the opportunity of this new land, since he was a trader and a cattleman. He came to Midland, Texas, in the winter of 1896 and liked what he saw. In the spring he sold his stock at auction and returned to Texas. His wife and sons followed him the next winter at Christmas.[300] The daughter Maude remained to finish her school year at Webb School in Bell Buckle.

Mrs. McKinley remembers her grandmother telling her of preparing lunches for the train ride from Bell Buckle to Midland. The Mississippi River was thirty miles wide as they crossed it. Their first home in Midland was on Marienfeld Street. Mr. Rankin traded this place for the King place on Kansas Street and 200 cows and calves from the 04 Ranch.

According to Mrs. McKinley, records show that he sold on August 5, 1899, to W. H. Cowden 400 head of stock cattle, branded F on the left loin and also young cattle branded F on the left shoulder. This stock was sold from the F. E. Rankin Ranch in Upton and Tom Green Counties, about fifty miles south of the town.[301]

John J. Terrell, Commissioner of the General Land Office, on May 8, 1907, certified that F. E. Rankin had lived three consecutive years on Section 26, Blk B, H. E. & W. T. Survey and also acquired Section 24 of Block B, H. E. & W. T. Survey;[302] also, that F. E. Rankin sold to the Orient Land Company the W½ of Section 24.[303]

Mrs. Rankin was indeed a pioneer since she was left alone much of the time and hauled her own supplies from Midland, which entailed a stop at Upland or at a rancher's house enroute.

Mr. Rankin was an extraordinary good shot and a keen trader. He was a great lover of animals, the care of which he often left to his wife.

Mr. F. E. Rankin died in 1916. Soon after his death, Mrs. Rankin opened up an insurance business in Midland and maintained her office in the National Bank Building during World War I. Mrs. Rankin spent the Depression years in Rankin. She then moved to Austin, where she kept house for her granddaughter, Elsie, while she was attending The University of Texas, and then came to McCamey where Elsie thaught school. She was living in Rankin at the time she became ill and moved back to Midland, where she passed away April 27, 1953, at the age of 91.[304]

SCHNAUBERT, MR. AND MRS. ARTHUR FRANCIS

Otto Schnaubert, who was educated in Germany to be a civil engineer, left his homeland in 1848. He came to Indianola, Texas, and became a naturalized citizen and married Marie Null. Arthur Francis was the fifth of their nine children.

Arthur recalled the Indianola Hurricane in 1875, after which their family moved to Cuero, where his father followed his profession and taught young men at night, preparing them to take college entrance examinations. In 1883 his father died. Arthur left Cuero with an older brother, an experienced trail driver, for Chihuahua, Mexico. From here they drove a herd of cattle to the open range for Curry Waller of Mc-Culloch County.

Arthur was employed for five years on the "S" Ranch near the junction of Salt Creek and the Colorado River. From this ranch he made cattle drives to New Mexico and to Kansas. In 1888 he went on a "Mule Drive" to Eddy, (Carlsbad) New Mexico, where the mules were delivered to contractors for railroad building.

On this trail near Pontoon Crossing, he carved the initials, "M.P. & A.S." When he returned to Waldrip, he married Miss Minnie Pool, aged 15, on December 23, 1891. With his bride they returned to a ranch at Panther Gap as foreman of the ranch. On December 30, 1891, Mr. Schnaubert made application to the County Surveyor of McCulloch County for a pre-emption certificate for 80 acres of land. This he occupied and improved for three years and was "entitled to the same as a homestead." This tract was patented November 12, 1895.

In 1899 Schnaubert concluded a contract with Billy Holmsey near Pontoon Crossing in Upton County. Here, he remained until 1904, where he drew a salary and had the privilege of running his own stock and building up his own herd. The Census of 1900 showed a population in Upton County of only 48 persons.[305]

In January of 1903 Mr. Schnaubert again changed his location when he accepted a contract with John R. Johnson as foreman for the John R. Johnson Ranch, with a dugout 3½ miles south of Wild China Pond. Here the Schnauberts moved their belongings with their seven children. The parents decided to hire a governess, arrange for a school-house and have the ranch school at their home. The cowboys helped Schnaubert convert a bunk house into a school building. Textbooks were furnished by the pupils. They were taught the first year by Miss Ruby Epps of Big Lake. She died in 1905. Early in 1906, Miss Lela Christy, a sixteen year old high school girl, was hired for the summer of 1906. She re-entered school in Garden City in September but married Duke Hill in the fall of that year. After she left, the Schnaubert children had no further schooling until 1909. Of this experience Mrs. Hill relates: "They were good children, and as I remember gave me no disciplinary problems. They liked school and did everything that I asked them to do willingly and never questioned my authority." Mrs. Schnaubert, a very gracious and hospitable ranch woman, did her best to make the young girl feel at home.[306]

In 1908 railroad land in Upton County was thrown open to settlers. Several settlers conferred with Schnaubert and planned to circulate a petition seeking to establish a school and organize the county. Schnaubert was designated to take the lead in circulating the petition, which was delivered to the Commissioners' Court in Midland. The Court immediately ordered a trustee election.

Upon the organization of the County in 1910, Schnaubert was elected Sheriff and Tax Collector. He was re-elected in 1912 and served until 1914.

The Sheriff and his wife were active in the organization of the Baptist Church in their home. Mr. Schnaubert served as Road Commissioner from 1914-1918. In 1920 he filled the unexpired term of the County Judge.

The Census of 1910 showed a population of 501. On account of the terrific drouth, by 1920 only 253 persons were left.[307] The three year drouth ruined the range. In 1916 Schnaubert and his sons headed their stock over 'Dobe Crossing across the Pecos for the Big Bend Country. The sons were sent back to school. When illness overcame this old patriarch, he headed for home. When his stock was herded up, he found that he had suffered great losses. His admonition to his children was, "Always pay your debts; tell the truth; always stay by your word." This drouth broke the old rancher.

Schnaubert, like a patriarch of old, suffered an even greater sorrow. The influenza epidemic took a heavy toll in his family in the death of the oldest son, Steve, and Steve's wife. The grandparents took their three young children, one of which was a baby just six days old, to rear. The elder Schnauberts had reared five sons and six daughters. Now with the death of their first-born and the responsibility of rearing three young children, they once again lifted up their eyes unto the hills.

Mr. Schnaubert moved to Carlsbad, New Mexico, where land was being opened up for settlement. In 1926 he was offered a job as "parts man" for the General Electric Company in Carlsbad. Meticulous in all phases of his work, he was never absent nor late in the 17 years of service. At the age of 70 he was retired on a pension. However, when World War II took so many younger men out of industry, Schnaubert asked his former employer to permit him to go back to work. He was given charge of the warehouse, where he worked until 1951.[308]

On December 23, 1954, the couple marked their 65th wedding anniversary. They celebrated the occasion in their home with a Christmas dinner party attended by several of their eight surviving children, 22 grandchildren and 41 great grandchildren.

Mr. Schnaubert came to the end of his life January 6, 1956. He was buried from the Carlsbad First Baptist Church at the Carlsbad Cemetery, January 8, 1956.[309] He was followed by his wife, who passed away December 4, 1956.

SMITH, DONALD C.

Donald C. Smith (First Lieutenant), was one of four crewmen who died when their C-130 crashed in flames a short distance from their airbase at Tuy Hoa, South Vietnam, December 20, 1965.[310]

This tragedy was exactly ten years after Smith turned in his freshman English autobiography at North Texas State University, December 20, 1955.[311]

Born August 27, 1937, in San Angelo, Texas, the son of Olin and Peggy (Gunnels) Smith, he moved with his family to Houston, Texas, where they remained a year. A care-free childhood, marked by the joy and the enthusiasm in youth in his many new experiences, endeared him to his classmates and to his teachers throughout his public school career. As a seventh grader, Smith enthusiastically helped his father in his welding shop; according to his autobigraphy, he wished to follow by becoming a mechanical engineer. He bypassed this freshman dream by majoring in government at N.T.S.U., graduating August 24, 1961.[312]

Immediately after graduation from college, Smith entered Officer Training School at Lackland Air Force Base. While in training, he married Miss Louise Gray, December 17, 1961.[313] Upon his graduation from Lackland, February, 1962, he was transferred to Moody Air Force Base, Georgia, from which he graduated March 27, 1963.[314]

Awarded Silver Wings, he was promoted from Second to First Lieutenant. Following this he entered Survival School at Dyess Air Force Base at Abilene, Texas, after which he was transferred to Naha Air Base, Okinawa. From here he piloted a C-130 transport on a resupply mission from Nha Tang to Tuy-Hoa Air Base when his plane crashed.[315]

He is survived by his widow, a son, Gregory Erroll, and a daughter, Jennifer Lee.

Lieutenant Smith was awarded the Purple Heart and received the following citation to accompany the Award of Air Medal:

First Lieutenant Donald C. Smith distinguished himself by meritorious achievement while participating in sustained aerial flight as a combat crew member in Southeast Asia from April 1, 1965, to October 19, 1965. During this period outstanding airmanship and courage were exhibited in the successful accomplishment of important missions under extremely hazardous conditions including the continuous possibility of hostile groundfire. His highly professional efforts contributed materially to the mission of the United States Air Force in Southeast Asia. The professional ability and outstanding aerial accomplishments of Lieutenant Smith reflect great credit upon himself and the United States Air Force.[316]

STILWELL, ARTHUR E.

Arthur E. Stilwell, son of Charles H. and Mary (Pierson) Stilwell, was born in Rochester, New York, October 21, 1859. His grandfather, Hamblen Stilwell, who helped construct both the Erie Canal and the New York Central Railroad, passed on his experiences to his young grandson. From his grandfather, Arthur also received his knowledge of high finances and the railroad industry.[317]

He married Miss Jennie Wood, June 10, 1879. At the age of 27, he organized the M.K. & T. Trust Company in Kansas City for the ultimate purpose of financing a railroad, which he intended to build with the Southern Pacific and the Texas Pacific Railroads. He was successful in building the Kansas City, Pittsburgh, and Gulf Railroad in the 1890's.[318]

On February 10, 1900, at a banquet in his honor, Mr. Stilwell announced in confident tones: "I have designed a railroad that will be 1600 miles long but will bring the Pacific Ocean 400 miles nearer Kansas City, and Kansas City 1600 miles nearer to Central and South America." This was the idea that gave birth to the Kansas City, Mexico and Orient Railway.[319]

A. E. Stilwell and his partners, on May 15, 1901, in Kansas City, Missouri, formed a company called the Orient Land Company for the purpose of buying, platting into townsites, improving, leasing, selling and otherwise disposing of lands in the State of Texas.[320]

The right-of-way agent, R. L. McCoulley, First Vice President and right-of-way agent for the Panhandle and Gulf Railway Company on June 1, 1904, obtained a right-of-way 200 feet out of Section 24, Block B, H.E. & W.T. R. R. Survey for the Panhandle and Gulf Railway out of Public School Land in Upton County, State of Texas.[321] On April 7, 1911, F. E. Rankin sold to the Orient Land Company the W½ of Section 24.[322]

On October 5, 1911, the Trustees of the Orient Land Company sold to Kansas City, Mexico and Orient Railway Company a "strip of land," a right-of-way and station ground 300' in width across the W½ Section 24, Block B.[323]

A. E. Stilwell acquired control of the Panhandle and Gulf Railway Company, March 3, 1900. By charter amendments the company changed its name under Kansas laws to the Kansas City, Mexico and Orient Railroad Company. The domicile by another amendment was changed from Sweetwater to San Angelo, Texas.[324] This charter was legalized by the Mexican Government, April 30, 1900. It was designed to build a through-line from Kansas City across Kansas, Oklahoma, Texas and Mexico to Topolobampo on the Pacific Ocean at the mouth of the California Gulf about 1660 miles.[325]

Construction began in 1902 at Wichita, Kansas, reaching Sweetwater in 1907, San Angelo in 1909, Girvin in 1911 and Alpine in 1913.[326]

Mrs. L. P. (Hattie) Hinde related that Mr. Stilwell and his surveyors in 1910 stayed at Monument Ranch on the Spring Creek Draw in Irion County. Mrs. Hinde and her husband managed the ranch and offered a welcome to the freighters who came by the well-known landmark. Here, Mr. Stilwell and his crew found welcome. Mrs. Hinde and her husband furnished wagons and teams for the surveyors and other crewmen. Mrs. Hinde provided the meals for the men and would carry their food along with her little children to the location. In the afternoon she drove the wagon with stakes for the surveyors and the construction crews as far as Big Lake.[327]

By 1911, the surveyors were approaching and surveying in Upton County. Mrs. H. B. (Effie) Earnest related that ranchers were moving from Upland to the new townsite, Rankin. Here, they were lending every effort to raise "dumps" and clear the right-of-way for the trackage. Men and women sought work on the railroad.[328]

The company was forced into bankruptcy March 9, 1912, and continued in receivership or financial uncertainty until the Atchison, Topeka and Santa Fe Railroad Company acquired indirect control August 25, 1928, and direct control on October 9, 1929.[329]

Of the acquisition by the Santa Fe Stilwell paid this tribute: "The discovery of oil and other temporary developments revived hope regarding the future of the property. Under these circumstances, the officers and the directors of the Santa Fe System regarded the acquisition of the Orient Railroad authorized in our report in Finance Docket 6958, as a sound business enterprise. I hope future decades will demonstrate this to have been correct. Nevertheless, in taking over the Orient property, the Santa Fe System performed a public service of large import which must have brought a sense of relief to all concerned, as it did to me."[330]

Thus, ends Stilwell's design of the railroad that brought the Pacific Ocean 400 miles closer to Kansas City — the Kansas City, Mexico and Orient Railway. In retrospect he looked out over the wild, rough country that he had tamed. He left behind an image of a stalwart, persevering achiever, looking across that vast domain into the future.[331] Mr. Stilwell died in New York City in 1928.

UPTON, JOHN CUNNINGHAM

John C. Upton was born on a farm near Winchester, Franklin County, Tennessee, January 22, 1828. He was the son of John and Anna (Cunningham) Upton. Educated in the common schools of Franklin County and in the University of Lebanon, Tennessee, he left Tennessee at the age of twenty-two for California, where he stayed until 1859. In that year he came to Texas, where he managed his mother's plantation. His mother and brother, William Felton Upton, had moved to Texas in 1853.[332]

Early in 1861 he raised a company, was chosen Captain and went to the seat of war in Virginia. He was attached to the Fifth Texas Regiment of Hood's Brigade and was in numerous engagements of that brigade up to his death.[333] He immediately saw action. The battles, sieges and engagements that Col. Upton participated in prior to his death in the Second Battle of Manassas follow:

1. Potomac Defense Line, Virginia; Nov. 7, 1861-March 8, 1862.
2. Rappahannock Defense Line, Virginia, March 12-April 7, 1862.
3. Yorktown Warwick Defense Line, Virginia, April 15-May 4, 1862.
4. Battle of Eltham's Landing, Virginia, May 2, 1862.
5. Battle of Seven Pines, Virginia, May 31-June 1, 1862.
6. Skirmish at Totopotomy Creek, Virginia, June 26, 1862.
7. Battle of Gaines' Mill, Virginia, June 27, 1862.
8. Battle of Malvern Hill, Virginia, July 1, 1862.
9. Skirmish at Freeman's Ford, Virginia, August 22, 1862.
10. Skirmish at Thoroughfare Gap, Virginia, August 28, 1862.
11. Battle of Second Manassas, Virginia, August 29-30, 1862.[334]

Col. John C. Upton was promoted to the rank of Major after the Battle of Seven Pines and to the rank of Lt. Col. after the Battle of Malvern Hill.[335]

The heroic actions of Col. Upton are described in the records of General Hood:

I put my troops in motion in accordance with instructions from General Longstreet, forming his advance guard. I placed Lt. Col. Upton of the Fifth Texas in command of about 150 picked men from the Texas Brigade to act as skirmishers and instructed him to rapidly push the Federals in front. I stressed the importance of hastening to the support of General Jackson. . . . Here was achieved by the advance guard one of those military feats which is entitled to the admiration of every soldier. Col. Upton drove the Federals with such rapidity that General Longstreet sent me orders two or three times to halt, since his army was unable to keep within supporting distance of my forces. The gallant Upton was, indeed, pre-eminent in his sphere as an outpost officer.[336]

In his official report August 22-31, 1862, General Hood made the following statement:

Lt. Col. Upton of the Fifth Texas, in command of a party of Texas riflemen constituting the advance guard, coming up with the rear guard of the enemy before sunrise, this gallant and distinguished officer drove them before him so rapidly that halts would have to be made for the troops in the rear to rest. Many gallant officers and men fell upon this memorable field. And our country has cause to regret the loss of none of her sons more than Lt. Col. John C. Upton, Fifth, Texas.[337]

UPTON, WILLIAM FELTON

William Felton Upton was born near Winchester, Tennessee, August 30, 1832, son of John and Anna Cunningham Upton. At the age of 21 years he moved with his mother and family to farms in Colorado and Fayette Counties, Texas. He opened a store in High Hill, where his neighbors were Czecks, Germans and other Anglo-Americans. They found him a good neighbor.[338]

Mr. Upton enlisted in the Confederate Cavalry, October 10, 1861, and served throughout the war, stationed in Galveston in Bradford's Regiment, which was later combined with Mann's Regiment. He was promoted to Lt. Colonel and was paroled at Columbus, Texas, July 14, 1865.[339]

William Felton Upton served in the 11th (1866); the 16th (1879-1881); the 17th (1881-1883); the 18th (1883-1885) and the 19th (1885-1887) Legislatures of Texas from the 70th District of the State of Texas.

On August 6, 1866, Upton presented his credentials to the Legislature of Texas from the 70th District, but when the radicals in the Congress of the United States ordered its adjournment for the so-called reconstruction of Texas, the Legislature was adjourned November 13, 1866.[340]

Mr. Upton rendered no further public service until 1879. In the meantime, he engaged in the general merchandise business with his partner, Mr. J. Matula of Schulenburg, Texas, and managed his farming interests and that of his mother.

In the 16th Legislature (1879-1881) Mr. Upton presented his credentials from the 70th District of the State of Texas, and thereafter he served successively through the 19th Legislature, a period of time when the State experienced economic, industrial and educational growth.[341]

During this period Hon. Upton served as Chairman of the Committee on Finance, on the Committee on Revenue and Taxation, and when the House of Representatives was in an uproar, he served as Chairman of the Whole House. He was called upon numerous occasions to serve as Speaker, Pro-tem.[342]

William Felton Upton died on February 7, 1887, in Schulenburg, Texas, where there is a large monument marking his grave. He was survived by his wife, Anne Henderson, who died in 1901.[343]

On February 8, 1887, the Hon. Will Lambert, Chief Clerk of the 20th Legislature, addressed the House of Representatives, saying: "True and loyal to his friends, firm in his convictions of right and wrong, but always conservative and liberal in his ideas of State policy, Col. Upton won for himself a name that will go down to posterity as one honored most by an admiring constituency. The impress of his wisdom shines resplendent upon the pages of the laws of the 11th, 16th, 17th, 18th and

*Mayer Halff (1836-1905) was a cattle-
man who headquartered in San Antonio.
He operated on the open range and had
holdings in Upton County.*

*Rachel Hart Halff (1848-1919) accom-
panied her husband many times up the
trail. Their ranching interests stretched
from Buchel County to Pecos County.*

*Henry M. Halff (1874-1934) was a
member of his father's firm, M. Halff
and Son. In 1908 he dedicated Upland
for the county seat of Upton County.
His office, located in Midland, is pictured at right.*

HENRY M. HALFF
LAND & LIVESTOCK.

Mr. Halff's Office at Midland.

Myra Halff, son of Mr. and Mrs. Henry M. Halff, was one year old when he was posed for this 1908 photo.

Round-up on the John T. McElroy Ranch, Upton County, 1930. In the picture are Fount Armstrong, Buck Kelton, and others from the "Y" Ranch.

Theodore Willis Johnson is pictured in this 1918 photograph.

The Old Rock House, built by Dr. George Elliott in 1883, was the first house in Upton County. Located six miles north of Rankin, it is the birthplace of Upton, for within the structure the election was held to create Upton County.

The Mesquite

EMBLEM OF THE UPTON COUNTY HISTORICAL SOCIETY

The mesquite, carefully examined, is of rare symmetrical value. The delicate leaves return each spring, the green to the vast emptiness, indicating the immemorial emblem of hope, contrasted by the harsh spike of thorn so similar to that which, some twenty centuries ago, pierced the brow of the Hope of the World. It is related to the deep-rooted Acacia, which itself is allegorical of the discovery of that which is lost. Then, the filigree-like blossom bears forth to provide for the future. With these in mind, I saw an emblem of the search for the past, recording the present, for those of the future.

—*Clyde Heron*

19th Legislatures, and will last as an enduring tribute to his sagacity and genius."[344]

In the same journal the Committee, appointed to draft a suitable resolution, submitted the following:

Austin, Texas, February 9, 1887

Hon. Geo. C. Pendeleton, Speaker of the House of Representatives:

Sir: Your Committee to whom was referred resolution touching the death of Hon. Wm. F. Upton with instruction to draft resolutions expressive of the House, beg leave to submit the following with the request that the same be spread upon the Journal:

'Whereas, the sad intelligence has been received of the death of the Hon. Wm. F. Upton of Fayette County, and,

Whereas, he has by a long life of devotion to his country and to his fellow man, his courage as a soldier, his wise judgment and conservative action as a Legislator, and his great heartedness, nobility of character and simplicity of life, endeared himself to his neighbors, friends and the people of the State; therefore, be it resolved:

1. That in the death of this distinguished citizen, the State has lost a wise Legislator, a good man and a worthy examplar of those manly virtues which dignify the State and ennoble the citizen;

2. That these resolutions be spread upon the Journals of the House, and a copy of the same be transmitted to his bereaved family.

More, Travis County
Page, Houston County
Camp, Limestone County
Committee[345]

YATES, IRA G.

Ira G. Yates was born in Hopkins County, Texas, October 29, 1859, and died in the Seton Infirmary at Austin, Texas, April 12, 1939.[346]

By his industry and by his principles by which he lived, Ira G. Yates became one of the richest men in Texas. As a child, he dug peanuts at fifty cents a day in Wilson County. At the age of twelve, he became a cowboy and at nineteen, a drover. He bought cattle in South Texas and speculated in horses.

After his marriage in 1883, he moved to San Angelo, where he served one term as City Marshall in 1889.

Yates and Louis Farr were partners in the ranching industry in Sterling County.[347]

Mr. Yates moved to Rankin in 1912, where he took an active part in community life, serving on the school board, helping to build a community church and building his own home there.

In 1913 he and L. L. Farr bought the Billy Holmsley Ranch, 12 miles south of Rankin. This ranch lay partly in Upton and partly in Crockett

Counties. The first business venture of Yates was trading 216 cattle to John R. Johnson for a lumberyard and a general merchandise store. Then, he traded the mercantile property in 1915 in part consideration for 16,540 acres in Pecos County from T. F. Hickox.[348]

Yates and his family spent eleven lean years on this parched property trying to keep his herd together. When prices of cattle began to decline, he went to San Angelo and located Levi Smith, an official in Mike Benedum's Trans Continental Oil Company, a successful operator in the Big Lake Field. Yates told Smith that he would lease his land, but, "I want to lease it to you."[349]

Smith offered him little encouragement, but the persistence of Yates finally won Smith over to drill a well on the ranch after Benedum had read encouraging reports from his own geologists. The well blew in October 28, 1926, the Number 1-A. Yates, and flowed 450 barrels a day. When it was deepened, it flowed 2,100 barrels an hour, and still later, 72,000 barrels a day. No. 30-A. Yates flowed 200,000 barrels a day, to become the largest gusher in the world.[350]

Thus, the struggling rancher Ira Yates became one of the richest men in Texas. When his field was outlined, it covered more than 25,000 acres. 500 wells still flow under natural pressure of the 632 wells that were drilled, with only 27 wells that have been abandoned.[351]

Other large oil fields have been found since 1928. In its day, though, the production was so outstandingly great that the operators soon saw it would be necessary to limit its production. So, here was the birth of the voluntary proration plan created by operators to bring about the orderly development of the field. This group recommended the most efficient methods of drilling, completing and producing wells and practices for the conservation of oil and gas. Thus, the Yates became known as the "Mother of Proration," a system which has become standard in the industry and which has conserved unknown millions of barrels of the nation's valuable oil resources.[352]

When news spread so quickly, oil scouts and lease brokers rushed to Rankin, and virtually overnight, crowds so overran the town that there were no facilities to house the visitors.

Thus, Yates saw the need for a hotel and announced that he would see that Rankin would have the best structure between Fort Worth and El Paso. He engaged an Abilene architect, C. C. Holder, to complete the plans. Quickly, the plans called for a three-story, 42-room to be built of brick and concrete.

No structure in the oil rich Permian Basin had so prominent a part in the oil development of West Texas. The State Historical Medallion that adorns the Yates Hotel distinguishes this as a structure deserving a page in oil history of this Permian History.[353]

The philanthropies of Mr. Yates have continued to benefit West Texas. He and his wife contributed to civic and church organizations. After the death of his wife, Mr. Yates built in her memory the Salvation Annie Yates Memorial Citadel in San Angelo; the Yates Hall at Camp Louis Farr for the Concho Valley Boy Scouts. He also donated a 29 acre campsite for Boy Scouts on the Pecos River near Iraan.[354]

Services for Ira George Yates were held in the First Methodist Church, San Angelo, Texas, on April 13, 1939, by Dr. K. P. Barton, Pastor, and Rev. Elmer Henson, Pastor of the First Christian Church. Internment was at Fairmount Cemetery, San Angelo, Texas.[355]

REFERENCES

CHAPTER I

1 J. A. Udden, Director Bureau of Economic Geology, University of Texas, Survey 1919; Interior Geological Survey, Washington, D.C., 1964; Cecil Gill, Humble Oil and Refining Company. Contour Map of Upton County, Mendoza Trail Museum, McCamey, Texas.

2 J. E. Hutchison, Texas Agricultural and Mechanical College of Texas, *Know Your Grasses* (no date). Tommie Johnson, a third generation rancher in Upton County, identified grasses in "Vegetational Areas of Texas." Upton County lies in Areas 7 and 10 as of March 15, 1965.

3 A. B. Conner, Texas Agricultural Experiment Station, *Catalogue of the Flora of Texas*, Bulletin 550 (July 1937), Division of Botany and Division of Agriculture.

4 Waterman Ormsby, *The Butterfield Overland Mail* (edited by Lyle H. Wright and Josephine Bynum), The Huntington Library, San Marino, California, 1955, p. 65.

5 Roscoe Conkling and Margaret Conkling, *The Butterfield Overland Mail 1857-1869*, Glendale, California, The Arthur Clark Co., Vol. I, page 370.

6 A. B. Conner, *Catalogue of the Flora of Texas*, Texas Agricultural Experiment Station, Bulletin 550, pages 73 and 74.

7 B. C. Tharp, *Texas Range Grasses*, p. 68.

8 U.S. Department of Commerce Weather Bureau, F. W. Reichelderfer, Chief, *Climatography of United States*, No. 11-36, McCamey, Texas, p. 67.

9 A. B. Conner, *Catalogue Valuable Plants Native to Texas*, Bulletin 551.

10 Robert M. White, U.S. Department of Commerce, Weather Bureau, *Climatography of the U.S.*, No. 86-36. Supplement for 1951-1960. McCamey, Texas, p. 49.

11 Charles E. Resser, *Shelled Creatures and Geological History*, Smithsonian Series, Vol. X, Ch. 5, p. 48; Sinclair Motor Oil Co., "Geologic Time Chart."

12 Paul Bartch, *Shelled Creatures and Geological History*, Vol. X, Part III, Ch. 1, p. 225.

13 Ray S. Bassler, *Shelled Creatures and Geologic History*, Smithsonian Series, Vol. X, Part I, p. 62; also Sinclair Motor Oil Company, "Geologic Time Chart."

14 W. T. Carter, *Reconnaissance of West Central Texas Soil Survey*, pp. 2124-2125.

CHAPTER II

15 Frank H. H. Roberts, "The Early Americans," *Scientific American*, February, 1951, p. 15.

16 N. Ethie Eagleton, "Deserts, Dunes and Mesas," *The Naturalist*, Vol. XII, No. 2, pp. 30-31.

17 J. E. Pearce, Ed., *Annual Report of the W.P.A. and The University of Texas Archaelogical Research*, p. 98.

18 Eagleton, "Deserts, Dunes and Mesas," *The Naturalist*, Vol. XII, No. 2, p. 31.

19 Carlos E. Castenado, *Our Catholic Heritage in Texas*, Vol. V, pp. 312-313.

20 *Ibid.*

21 Mary Sue (Jackson) Bandy, "The Jediondas Greet Mendoza," *Junior Historian*, Vol. XVI, No. 1, p. 24.

22 Walter Prescott Webb, *The Great Plains*, p. 135.

23 Barbara (Johnson) Porter, "Early Trails in the Upton County Area," *Junior Historian*, Vol. XVII, No. 4, p. 23.

24 *Ibid.*

25 Kenneth F. Neighbors, "The Expedition of Major Robert S. Neighbors to El Paso in 1849," *The Southwest Historical Quarterly*, Vol. LVIII, p. 38.

26 Dr. James Day, "Castle Gap Dedication," May 25, 1968.

27 Bobby McKinney, "The Butterfield Trail Through Texas," *Junior Historian*, Vol. XVIII, No. 2, p. 2.

28 A photostatic copy of this charter, to be found in the Pecos County Clerk's Office, is framed in the Mendoza Trail Museum in Upton County; W. R. Baggett, "Early Day Irrigation Ditches on the Pecos," *Frontier Times*, July, 1942; Bascom Giles, *History and Disposition of the Texas Public Domain*, Austin, 1945, p. 12.

29 Antonio Lopez de Santa Anna, *The Mexican Side of the Texas Revolution* (translated by Carlos Castenado) pp. 319-320; Z. T. Fulmore, *The History and Geography of Texas*, p. 278.

30 Mittendorfer, *Map of Texas*, 1874.

31 *Handbook of Texas*, Vol. I, p. 598.

32 Mittendorfer, Publisher, *Map of Texas Exhibiting Minerals and Agricultural Districts, Post Offices and Mail Routes, Timberland, Prairies and Swamp Land*, Philadelphia, 1874.

33 Green Peyton, *America's Heartland, The Southwest*, p. 79.

34 Enoch Smith, "Castle Gap," *McCamey News*, June 24, 1965, p. 4; Dr. James Day, "Castle Gap Park Dedication," May 25, 1968.

35 Ronald Baron, "Canyon Creed," *Junior Historian*, Vol. XIII, No. 5, p. 29.

36 B. B. Paddock, "J. Wright Mooar, *History and Biographical Record of North and West Texas*, Vol. I, p. 247.

37 N. Ethie Eagleton, "An Historic Indian Cache in Pecos County," *Bulletin of the Texas Archaeological Society*, Vol. 26, pp. 200-217. 1955.

38 *Upton County Deed Records*, Vol. I, p. 88; Upton County Deed Records, Vol. IV, p. 264.

39 *Ibid.*, Vol. I, pp. 88, 92 & 93.

40 *Ibid.*, Vol. I, p. 125.

41 *Texas Almanac 1966-1967*, p. 414.

42 B. B. Inghram to N. E. E., October 20, 1967.

43 *Midland County Deed Records*, Book I, pp. 239-250; *Brewster County Deed Records*, Vol. VII, p. 349; *Buchel County Deed Records*, No. I, p. 164.

44 Yvonne (Johnson) Selby, "Dobe Crossing," *Junior Historian*, Vol. V, No. 4, p. 2.

45 *Ibid.*, p. 3.

46 Dee Locklin to N. E. E., April 18, 1967.

47 Josie (Schnaubert) Brown, "Arthur Francis Schnaubert," *Junior Historian*, Vol. 9, No. 6, p. 25.

CHAPTER III

48 Z. T. Fulmore, *The History and Geography of Texas, as told in County Names,* p. 261.

49 R. M. Hale, Commissioner of the General Land Office, *Map of Upton County,* 1889.

50 *Texas Almanac 1966-1967,* p. 132.

51 Josie (Schnaubert) Brown, "Arthur Francis Schnaubert," *Junior Historian,* Vol. IX, No. 6, p. 26.

52 *Texas Almanac 1966-1967,* p. 414; Yvonne (Johnson) Selby, "The 'Dobe Crossing," *Junior Historian,* Vol. V, No. 4, p. 4

53 J. T. Robinson, Commissioner, *Report of the Commissioner of the General Land Office, 1918-1920,* p. 43.

54 *Upton County Deed Records,* Vol. X, p. 528.

55 Mrs. Henry Earnest to N. E. E., May 20, 1963. Mrs. Earnest moved to Upton County in 1903.

56 Miss Flossie Coats, *San Angelo Standard Times,* March 2, 1965, Sec. B, p. 1.

57 Mrs. Bess Moorman, "Notes."

58 *Records of the General Services Administration,* National Archives and Records Service, Washington, D.C., courtesy of Hon. O. C. Fisher, Texas 21st District, United States Congress.

59 Dave Price to N. E. E., June 10, 1965.

60 Mrs. Henry Earnest to N. E. E., May 20, 1963.

61 *Midland, the Queen City of the Plains,* Vol. I, No. 1, pp. 52-53.

62 Josie (Schnaubert) Brown, "Arthur Francis Schnaubert," *Junior Historian,* Vol. IX, No. 6, p. 27.

63 *Upton County Deed Records,* Vol. IV, p. 213.

64 *Ibid.,* Vol. V, p. 446.

65 *Ibid.,* Vol. V, p. 267 and Vol. VIII, p. 209.

66 *Ibid.,* Vol. VIII, p. 370.

67 Frank Davis, "Upton County Historical Group Hears Damron City Report," *Midland Reporter-Telegram,* February 12, 1959.

68 *Minutes of the Commissioners' Court of Midland County,* Vol. II, pp. 527-528.

69 *Ibid.,* Vol. II, p. 541.

70 Mrs. Henry Earnest to N. E. E., May 20, 1963.

71 *The Texas Almanac, 1966-1967,* p. 132.

72 *Records of the General Services Administration,* National Archives and Records Service, Washington, D.C., Courtesy of Hon. O. C. Fisher, Texas 21st District, U. S. Congress.

73 Dave Price to N. E. E., July 15, 1965.

74 Mrs. Dave Price to N. E. E., July 15, 1965.

75 Dave Price to N. E. E., July 16, 1965.

76 *Minutes of the Commissioners' Court of Upton County,* Vol. I, p. 98.

77 *Delinquent Tax Book No. 1,* Upton County.

78 Josie (Schnaubert) Brown, "Arthur Francis Schnaubert," *Junior Historian,* Vol. IX, No. 6, p. 28.

79 *Minutes of the Commissioners' Court of Upton County*, Vol. I, p. 102.

80 *Ibid.*, Vol. I, p. 102.

81 *Ibid.*, Vol. I, p. 146.

82 Josie (Schnaubert) Brown, "Arthur Francis Schnaubert," *Junior Historian*, Vol. IX, No. 6, p. 29.

CHAPTER IV

83 *Texas Almanac, 1966-1967*, p. 132

84 Mrs. Henry Earnest to N. E. E., July 20, 1963.

85 *Upton County Deed Records*, Vol. X, p. 338.

86 *Ibid.*, Vol. X, p. 479.

87 Elmer Kelton, in a taped interview with Mr. Newland. Throughout the tapes can be heard the clanking of an old windmill a short distance away, August 23, 1964.

88 *Minutes of the Commissioners' Court*, Vol. I, p. 64.

89 *Records of the General Services Administration*, National Archives and Records Service, Washington, D.C., Courtesy of Hon. O. C. Fisher, Texas 21st District, U.S. Congress, February 7, 1967.

90 *Minutes of the Commissioners' Court*, Book I, p. 70.

91 *Ibid.*, Book I, p. 100.

92 *Ibid.*, Book I, p. 131.

93 Peggy (Dossey) Garner, "Early Days in Upton County," *Junior Historian*, March, 1948, Vol. VIII, No. 5, p. 6.

94 Mrs. Bess Moorman, "Notes," Ira L. Parrack was pastor of the First Baptist Church at Chillicothe, Texas. His letter to Mrs. Moorman was dated April 18, 1942.

95 Peggy (Dossey) Garner, "Early Days in Upton County," *Junior Historian*, Vol. VIII, p. 12; LuAnn Kelton, "Christmas On The Pecos," *Junior Historian*, December, 1964, Vol. XXV, No. 3, p. 1.

96 Josie (Schnaubert) Brown, "Arthur Francis Schnaubert," *Junior Historian*, Vol. IX, No. 6, p. 29, May 1949.

97 Iona (Poole) Moore, "In the Days of Crap-Shooter," *Junior Historian*, Vol. VI, No. 5, p. 4.

98 Mr. and Mrs. V. G. Nevill, a tape recording of their experiences from 1905-1966 for the McCamey Women's Study Club.

99 Mrs. Bess Moorman, "Notes," from Ed Schnaubert and Duke Hill.

100 Mrs. Jack Smith, Secretary-Treasurer, Upton County Historical Society.

101 Peggy (Dossey) Garner, "Early Days in Upton County," *Junior Historian*, Vol. VIII, p. 7.

102 *Rankin News*, May 26, 1960, Vol. XXXV, No. 31.

103 Mrs. Opal Nix, Rankin, Texas, December 9, 1965; J. A. Udden, Director Bureau of Economic Geology and Technology, University of Texas, Southwest Upton County, Surveyed 1919.

104 E. F. Cummings, Rankin Water Superintendent, September 27, 1968.

105 Minutes of the Upton County Commissioners' Court, Vol. IV, p. 107.

106 *Ibid.*, April 21, 1915, Vol. I, p. 131.

107 Rena Elizabeth McQuary, "An Educational Survey of Upton County, 1904-

1944," a thesis presented to the Faculty of the Graduate School of Hardin-Simmons University.

[108] *Ibid.*, p. 27.

[109] Clara M. Parker, *Annie Webb Blanton, Founder of the Delta Kappa Gamma Society*, pp. 22-23.

[110] Don Jones, "Dr. Homer Powers, A Pioneer Physician," *Junior Historian*, January, 1954, Vol. XIV, No. 4, p. 19.

[111] McQuary, "An Educational Survey in Upton County, 1904-1944."

[112] Miss Allie V. Scott to N. E. E., September 13, 1968.

[113] *Marathon World*, Marathon Oil Company, Winter 1966, pp. 18-19.

[114] *Ibid.*, p. 19.

[115] *The Rankin (Texas) News,* Thursday October 13, 1966. (No page numbers).

[116] Dunn Lowery, President, First State Bank, Rankin, Texas, to George Ramer, September, 11, 1968.

[117] McQuary, "An Educational Survey of Upton County, 1904-1944," pp. 31-32.

[118] *Ibid.*, p. 33.

[119] H. G. Adams, Superintendent, Rankin Schools, to N. E. E., September 11, 1968.

[120] *Records of the General Services Administration*, National Archives and Records Service, Washington, D.C., Courtesy of Hon. O. C. Fisher, Texas 21 District United States Congress, March 21, 1967.

[121] *Upton County Deed Records*, Vol. XX, p. 77.

[122] *Records of the General Services Administration*, National Archives and Records Service, Washington, D.C., Courtesy of Hon. O. C. Fisher, Texas 21 District United States Congress, February 7, 1967.

[123] Mrs. Opal Nix, to the Upton County Historical Society, September 12, 1958.

[124] Bernice (Muschalek) Hurst, "The Young Town of McCamey," *Junior Historian*, Vol. VII, No. 3, p. 13, December, 1946.

[125] O. W. Williams, *The Personal Narrative*, edited by S. D. Myres, El Paso, Texas, Texas Western Press, pp. 314-315.

[126] Bill Collyns, former staff writer, *McCamey News*, April 27, 1934, p. 1.

[127] *Upton County Deed Records*, Vol. XXVI, p. 584.

[128] *McCamey News*, June 23, 1960, p. 4.

[129] Elizabeth (Cope) Hamilton, "McCamey's Water Supply," *Junior Historian*, Vol. V, No. 1, p. 11, September, 1944.

[130] George Ramer to N. E. E., September 17, 1968.

[131] Jim Pirkle, Water Supt. Water Dept., "A Report to the People, City of McCamey," October 1, 1966, through September 30, 1967, p. 11.

[132] *Ibid.*, Oct. 1, 1964 through Sept. 30, 1965, p. 3.

[133] *Ibid.*, Oct. 1966-Sept. 1967, p. 19.

[134] *Records of the General Services Administration*, National Archives and Records Service, Feb. 6, 1967.

[135] Burton Lingo Right-of-Way Lease from K.C.M.&O. Ry. Co. of Texas, Oct. 21, 1927.

[136] "The Hub of the Oil Fields," *Directory of the City of McCamey*, 1929, Business Directory of McCamey, Texas.

137 *Ibid.,* p. 5.

138 Henrietta M. Larson and Kenneth Wiggins Porter, *History of the Humble Oil and Refining Company,* Harper and Brothers, p. 196.

139 *Ibid.,* p. 235.

140 *McCamey News,* May 13, 1938, p. 9.

141 *Ibid.,* June 24, 1965, p. 2.

142 Eddie Halamicek, "Slicker Slithers In," *Junior Historian,* May, 1953, No. 6, p. 23.

143 Mr. and Mrs. Dee Locklin to N. E. E., September 15, 1967.

144 Billy Locklin, "Coyotes and No Fences," *Junior Historian,* May, 1955, Vol. XV, No. 6, p. 4.

145 M. E. Pittman, *West Texas Today,* July, 1939. The official publication of the West Texas Chamber of Commerce.

146 *The McCamey News,* August 18, 1950, Vol. XXV, No. 34, Sec. III, p. 8.

147 *Ibid.,* June 23, 1955, Sec. IV, p. 1.

148 Derwood Langston, President of McCamey Security State Bank, to N. E. E., March 30, 1968.

149 *San Angelo Standard Times,* May 22, 1960, p. 7B.

150 *McCamey News,* June 23, 1955, Vol. 30, No. 25, Sec. III, p. 3.

151 Catherine B. Dod, "History of Education in Upton County," p. 80.

152 Rena McQuary, "An Educational Survey of Upton County, 1904-1944," pp. 40-41.

153 *Ibid.,* p. 44.

154 *Ibid.,* pp. 45-46, J. A. Phillips Company, Special Examination McCamey Independent School District, McCamey, Texas, Nov. 15, 1928, p. 1.

155 *Ibid.,* p. 46.

156 C. V. Compton to Rena McQuary, July 21, 1944, p. 47.

157 *Ibid.,* p. 48.

158 *Ibid.,* in McQuary's "An Educational Survey of Upton County, 1904-1944," p. 49.

159 *The Badger,* October 21, 1929, Vol. 1, p. 2.

160 Bill Collyns, *McCamey News,* April 27, 1934, Vol. 8, No. 35.

161 McQuary, "An Educational Survey of Upton County, 1904-1944," p. 49.

162 *Ibid.,* p. 50.

163 Bill Collyns' "City's Early Growth," *McCamey News,* April 27, 1934, Vol. VIII, No. 35.

164 *Minutes of the School Board of the McCamey Independent School District.* (No pages numbered.)

165 Mrs. Lillie Bell Brown, Secretary and Treasurer of the Social, Civic and Art Club, 1968.

166 Gertrude Smith, Secretary, Rankin Women's Study Club.

167 W. M. Day, Jr., Upton County Agricultural Agent, to N. E. E., September 19, 1968.

168 *San Angelo Standard Times,* September 26, 1966, Section D, p. 1.

169 Leon Feuge, Administrator of Rankin Hospital, to N. E. E., September 19, 1968.

170 Joe Collins, Administrator, McCamey Hospital, to N. E. E., September 11, 1968.

CHAPTER V

[171] Olive O. (Mrs. George B.) McCamey, "A Brief Biography of George B. Mc-Camey," January 30, 1968, a paper prepared for the author.

[172] "Oil Appreciation," *McCamey News*, Issue 1954, p. 1.

[173] *San Angelo Standard Times*, San Angelo, Texas, May 28, 1967.

[174] Lee Watson, *San Angelo Standard Times*, June 28, 1960.

[175] Mr. Jim Smith to N.E.E., June 15, 1965.

[176] *Deed Records of Upton County, Texas*, Vol. 20, pp. 23 and 124.

[177] Mrs. George Ramer to the author, April 15, 1968.

[178] Rena Elizabeth McQuary, "An Educational Survey of Upton County, 1904-1944," p. 50.

[179] Henrietta M. Larson and Kenneth Wiggins Porter, *History of the Humble Oil and Refining Company*, 1959, pp. 189; 196; 235; 545 and 601. "Oil in the Permian Basin," *The Humble Way*, January-February, 1947, pp. 8-15. *Ibid.*

[180] *Pecos County Deed Records*, Vol. 95, p. 195.

[181] Amos Floyd and Arthur Caldwell II to the author, July 27, 1965.

[182] L. H. Byrd, Division Manager for Humble Oil and Refining Company located in Midland, Texas, "Remarks at the Dedication of the Historical Marker at the McCamey Campsite of Humble," October 29, 1967.

[183] B. A. Epley, Mayor of the City of McCamey, October 29, 1967.

[184] George Ramer to the author, July 8, 1968. An unnamed and undated newspaper clipping in the Upton County Archives.

[185] "Report of the McCamey Junior Historian," *The Junior Historian*, Vol. XVII, No. 5, p. 31.

[186] Arthur Caldwell III, "Mike Benedum and the Permian Basin," *Junior Historian*, Vol. XVII, No. 5, p. 3. "The Two Million Western Acres," *The Daily Texan*, Nov. 2, 1930.

[187] *Ibid.*, p. 5.

[188] *Ibid.*

[189] *Ibid.*

[190] Sam Mallison, *The Great Wildcatter, The Story of Mike Benedum*, pp. 338; 451; 461.

[191] Weir No. 1. Inscription appears on the Texas State Highway Marker, 7 miles from the forks of Highway 67 and Highway 329, Upton County.

[192] Highway Marker Weir No. 1 — the inscription appearing on the marker seven miles from the intersection of Highway 67 and Highway 329, Texas State Historical Survey Committee.

[193] *1967 Upton County Tax Records*, Upton County, Texas.

[194] *1968 Upton County Tax Records*, Upton County, Texas.

[195] Howard Wolf, "Back to the ABC's," *Junior Historian*, December 1951, Vol. XII, No. 3, pp. 19-20.

[196] Mrs. A. L. Andrew, "A Paper Presented to the McCamey Women's Study Club," February, 1964.

[197] *Upton County Tax Rolls for 1967*.

[198] "Oil Production in Upton County Reaches 360 Million Barrels," *McCamey News*, December 15, 1966.

References

References 93

199 "El Paso Natural Gas Opens Lines to Midkiff Installation," _San Angelo Standard Times_, October 15, 1954, page 1-B.

200 _Texas Almanac, 1966-1967_, p. 473.

201 N. Ethie Eagleton, "The Significance of the Pecos River in Native Cultures," a research paper submitted in July, 1955, to fulfill the requirements of Sul Ross State College History Department, Dr. Clifford B. Casey, Teacher.

CHAPTER VI

202 _Claude Worthington Benedum Foundation_, pp. 11-12.

203 _Ibid._

204 Arthur Caldwell III, "Mike Benedum and the Permian Basin," _Junior Historian_, Vol. XVII, No. 5, p. 4.

205 Jim C. Langdon to N. E. E., October 6, 1964.

206 "World Famous Wildcatter Still Active at 89 Years," _San Angelo Standard Times_, July 6, 1958.

207 _Claude Worthington Benedum Foundation_, p. 12.

208 Darrel Freeman, _The McCamey News_, May 26, 1960.

209 Bureau of Vital Statistics, Texas Dept. of Health No. 223.

210 The Liner, May 1966; Vol. V, Humble Pipe Line Company, Houston.

211 _Big Lake Wildcat_, May 5, 1966.

212 Jimmy Martin, _West Texas Electric Times_, February, 1950, p. 3.

213 "Three Managers Directed W.T.U. McCamey Operations," _The McCamey News_, August 18, 1950, Section III, p. 8.

214 _Minutes of the McCamey Independent School Board_, April 21, 1941; 1942; April 9, 1947; July 5, 1949; October 12, 1949; November 9, 1949; January 11, 1950. (No page numbers.)

215 John Cole to N. E. E., October 12, 1968.

216 Mrs. Effie Earnest to N. E. E., July 20, 1963.

217 Peggy Sue Garner, "Early Days in Upton County," _Junior Historian_, Vol. VIII, No. 5, p. 4.

218 Mrs. Opal Nix and other members of the Upton County Historical Society to N. E. E., June 16, 1967.

219 "Rankin Resident Dies in San Angelo," _The San Angelo Standard Times_, June 19, 1966.

220 James Cox, _Historical and Biographical Record of the Cattle Industry and Cattlemen of Texas and Adjacent Territory_, p. 462.

221 _Ibid._ Richard G. Santos, Bexar County Archives, San Antonio, Texas, to N. E. E., July 20, 1965.

222 _Upton County Deed Records_, Vol. 1, pp. 88 & 92; Vol. 4, p. 264; and Vol. 12, p. 223.

223 John Howard Griffin, _The Land of the High Sky_, p. 112.

224 _Midland Reporter-Telegram_, October 18, 1953.

225 Patricia Chadwell, Head of Southwest and Genealogy Department, Fort Worth Public Library, to N. E. E., October 22, 1965. George W. Elliott III to N. E. E., October 22, 1965.

226 Mrs. Jack Garner, manuscript.

227 Fred Gipson, "John Garner Has Raised Horses And He's Still in the Business," undated *San Angelo Standard Times,* page 10.

228 *McCamey News,* Ed Halamicek, January 27, 1954.

229 M. H. Halff, Richardson, Texas, to N. E. E., October 22, 1964.

230 *Upton County Deed Records,* Rankin, Texas, Vol. 61, p. 563.

231 Allie V. Scott, a retired school teacher in the Midland Schools, who was frequently a guest in the Halff home, 1914-1918, to N. E. E., April 20, 1965.

232 Grace Miller White, "The Activities of M. Halff and Brother," *Frontier Times,* San Antonio, Public Library, Vol. XIX, p. 169.

233 Dave Price personal interview with N. E. E., September 16, 1963.

234 M. H. Halff, Richardson, Texas, to N. E. E., October 22, 1964.

235 Ernestine (Halff) Freeman to N. E. E., September 9, 1963.

236 *Ibid.,* October 22, 1964.

237 White, Grace Miller, "The Activities of M. Halff and Brother," *Frontier Times,* Vol. XIX, p. 169.

238 White, John H. "Cap," "The Activities of M. Halff and Brother," Manuscript for G. A. C. Halff.

239 Grace Miller White, *Frontier Times,* Vol. XIX, p. 170.

240 *Buchel County Deed Records,* December 14, 1883, Vol. No. 1, p. 164.

241 *Crockett County Deed Records,* Vol. I, p. 391; Vol. II, pp. 95-98; Vol. 11B, p. 174; Vol. II, pp. 276; 378 & 350; Vol. VI, p. 450; Vol. VII, pp. 370 & 375, 415, 416; Vol. VIII, pp. 81, 110, 343, 111, 313, 508, 509; Vol. IX, p. 188; Vol. X, pp. 264, 361.

242 Grace Miller White, *Frontier Times,* Vol. XIX, p. 170.

243 Henry M. Hart, Vice Chairman of the Executive Committee of the Bank of Commerce of San Antonio to Mr. Derwood Langston, Security State Bank of McCamey, April 2, 1965; Richard Santos, Bexar County Archives, to N. E. E., December 16, 1964.

244 Mrs. Norman (Ernestine Halff) Freeman to N. E. E., October 18, 1965.

245 Mrs. Harris' account told many times to N. E. E.

246 George Ramer, Mrs. Harris' longtime friend.

247 Mrs. Harris' own account as told to N. E. E.

248 *Minutes of the McCamey Women's Study Club,* 1929.

249 *McCamey Women's Study Club Yearbooks,* 1929-1930; 1930-1931; 1932-1933; 1942-1943; 1943-1944; 1944-1945.

250 N. Ethie Eagleton, *The McCamey News,* January 2, 1965.

251 The Johnson Family Bible.

252 Yvonne (Johnson) Selby, "Dobe Crossing," *Junior Historian,* Vol. 5, No. 4, p. 1.

253 Mabel Howard, *Memoirs of Mr. and Mrs. John F. Lane,* unpublished.

254 *Minutes of the Commissioners' Court,* Vol. 1, p. 1.

255 Scotty Howard, a theme written in his history class, 1950, unpublished.

256 Olive O. (Mrs. George B.) McCamey, "A Brief Biography of George B. McCamey," January 30, 1968, prepared for N. E. E.

257 Official Texas Marker, Upton County, brought in December 6, 1961, Weir No. 1.

258 Dunn Lowery, President, First State Bank, Rankin, in Upton County, Sept. 11, 1968.

259 Allie V. Scott, *Memoirs of Margaret Littlejohn;* Miss Scott lived in an apartment adjoining Mrs. Littlejohn.

260 Kelly Crozier, *San Angelo Standard Times,* March 31, 1957.

261 Margaret (Mrs. E. C.) Bone, Mrs. Littlejohn's daughter.

262 Olive O. (Mrs. George B.) McCamey, "A Brief Biography of George B. McCamey," prepared for N. E. E., January 30, 1968, Fort Worth, Texas.

263 *Ibid.*

264 *Ibid.*

265 *Ibid.*

266 *Ibid.*

267 *Ibid.*

268 Ellis Arthur Davis, ed., *The Historical Encyclopedia of Texas,* I, pp. 298-299.

269 Olive O. McCamey, "A Brief Biography of George B. McCamey."

270 "Men of Texas," *The New Encyclopedia of Texas,* compiled and edited by Ellis A.Davis and Edwin H. Grobe, Vol. I, p. 526. (Courtesy of Mrs. Sue Navarro who photostated the article "John T. McElroy.") Hereafter, reference to Mrs. Navarro will be referred to as "Navarro Notes."

271 "Paul Patterson Speaks to Historical Society on History of McElroy (Jigger Y) Ranch," the *McCamey News,* December 20, 1962.

272 "Navarro Notes."

273 "Patterson Speaks to Historical Society on History of McElroy (Jigger Y) Ranch."

274 *The Texas Almanac, 1966-1967,* p. 414.

275 In 1950 Fred Dusterwick, an undergraduate student of Ohio State Univ., spent his summer working on the McElroy Ranch. As a research project, he tried his hand at writing "A History of the McElroy Ranch;" Edward J. Brook, Manager of the McElroy Ranch, sent to Edith Windham, November 20, 1964, a copy of Dusterwick's "A History of the McElroy Ranch," for the Upton County Archives. Hereafter, reference to this paper will be referred to as "Dusterwick's Notes."

276 *Ibid.*

277 *Ibid.*

278 *Pecos Enterprise,* October 16, 1936.

279 "Navarro Notes," *The New Encyclopedia of Texas,* Vol. I, p. 526.

280 Paul Patterson, "Patterson Speaks to the Upton County Historical Society on the History of the McElroy Ranch," *McCamey News,* December 20, 1962; *Upton County Deed Records,* Vol. I, pp. 313 & 387.

281 "Dusterwick's Notes."

282 *Upton County Deed Records,* Vol. 26, p. 421.

283 Mrs. Emmet Matejowsky to N. E. E., January 1, 1969.

284 Mrs. E. P. Halamicek, McCamey, Texas, to N. E. E., January 30, 1969.

285 Paul Patterson to N. E. E., June 14, 1967. Much of the following is taken from Paul Patterson's memories of his father, Judge Patterson.

286 *Ibid.*

287 *Ibid.*

288 "County Judge Services Held," *The McCamey News,* October 27, 1966.

289 Jimmy Martin, *West Texas Electric Times,* September 1950, p. 10.

290 "Funeral Rites Set Today for Pittman," *San Angelo Standard Times,* August 25, 1950, p. 12.

291 Martin, *West Texas Electric Times,* p. 10.

292 Aileen Gibson, to N. E. E., July 27, 1953.   293 *Ibid.*

294 Don Jones, "Dr. Homer Powers, a Pioneer Physician," *Junior Historian,* Vol. XIV, No. 4, p. 19.

295 County Clerk's Records, Upton County, Texas.

296 Miss Allie V. Scott, a Rankin teacher from 1918-1920, to N. E. E., July 30, 1953.

297 Don Jones, "Dr. Homer Powers, A Pioneer Physician," *Junior Historian,* Vol. XIV, No. 4, p. 19.

298 *Ibid.,* p. 31.

299 Nancy (Rankin) McKinley, June 9, 1966. Mrs. John P. (Nancy Rankin) Mc-Kinley, Chairman of District 8, Texas State Historical Survey Committee, presented a "Biographical Sketch of Finis Ewing and Eliza Rankin" to the Upton County Historical Society, June 9, 1966. She is the granddaughter of Mr. and Mrs. F. E. Rankin. Reference to her in this paper will be "Nancy McKinley Notes."

300 "Nancy McKinley Notes."

301 *Ibid.*   302 *Upton County Deed Records,* Vol. X, p. 495.

303 *Ibid.,* p. 338.   304 "Nancy McKinley Notes."

305 Josie (Schnaubert) Brown, "Arthur Francis Schnaubert," *Junior Historian,* Vol. IX, No. 6, pp. 25-26.

306 Rena Elizabeth McQuary, "An Educational Survey of Upton County, 1904-1944," a thesis presented to the Faculty of the Graduate School, Hardin-Simmons University, 1945.

307 *Texas Almanac,* 1966-1967, p. 132.

308 Josie (Schnaubert) Brown, "Arthur Francis Schnaubert," *Junior Historian,* Vol. IX, No. 6, p. 29.

309 N. Ethie Eagleton, "Arthur Francis Schnaubert Dies in New Mexico Hospital," *The McCamey News,* January 12, 1956.

310 Dyess Air Force Base Chapel Memorial Services, February 18, 1966, for Capt. Terry F. Katterhenry ,1st Lieutenant Donald C. Smith, Tech. Sgt. Wm. Crisp, and A.I.C. Willie J. Mitchell, Jr.

311 Don C. Smith, "Smith's Folly," N.T.S.U. English 103-2, Dec. 20, 1955.

312 "Final Tribute Paid 4 Ex-Dyess Men," *San Angelo Standard Times,* February 12, 1966, p. 2A.

313 Mrs. Olin Smith, Don Smith's mother, to N. E. E., July 10, 1967.

314 *San Angelo Standard Times,* February 12, 1966.   315 *Ibid.*

316 Department of the Air Force, Headquarters United States Air Force, Randolph Air Force Base, Texas.

317 John Broussard, "Arthur Stilwell's Dream City," *Junior Historian,* Vol. XXI, No. 3, p. 3.

318 *Ibid.*

319 James Marshall, *Santa Fe, the Railroad that Built An Empire,* p. 295.

320 *Upton County Deed Records,* Vol. X, p. 528.   321 *Ibid.,* Vol. 2, p. 142.

322 *Ibid.,* Vol. X, p. 338.   323 *Ibid.,* Vol. X, p. 484.

324 Arthur L. Carnahan, "Texas Collection," *Southwestern Historical Quarterly,* Vol. 54, p. 490.

325 *Ibid.,* Vol. 53, No. 4, pp. 479-481.　　326 *Ibid.,* Vol. 53, p. 481.

327 Mrs. Hattie Hinde to N. E. E., April 20, 1944. Confirmed by Crescendze Hinde, October 12, 1968.

328 Mrs. Henry Earnest to N. E. E., July, 1962.

329 Arthur L. Carnahan, "Texas Collection," Vol. LIV, No. 4, p. 491.

330 Lelyle (Harris) Russell, "The Kansas City, Mexico and Orient Railway Company of Texas," Manuscript, 1946.

331 George W. Ramer to N. E. E., October 12, 1968.

332 Arthur Caldwell III, "Upton County's Uptons," *Junior Historian,* Vol. XIX, No. 1, September, 1958.

333 Z. T. Fulmore, *The History and Geography of Texas As Told in County Names,* p. 261.

334 Col. H. B. Simpson to N. E. E., May 16, 1963. Col. Simpson is the author of *Gaines' Mill to Appomattox,* published by Texian Press.

335 General Services Administration, National Archives and Records Service, to N. E. E., May 16, 1963.

336 J. B. Hood, *Advance and Retreat,* p. 33.

337 J. B. Polley, *Hood's Texas Brigade,* p. 333.

338 Arthur Caldwell III, "Upton County's Uptons," *Junior Historian,* Vol. XIX, No. 1, September, 1958.

339 General Services Administration, National Archives and Records Service (39356) to N. E. E., May 16, 1963.

340 *Journal of the House of Representatives,* 11th Legislature.

341 James T. DeShields, *The Set in High Places,* p. 310.

342 *House Journals,* Texas House of Representatives 1879-1887; Legislature Records of Texas, 16th (1879-1880); 17th (1881-1882); 18th (1883-1884); 19th (1885-1886); *Legislative Manual,* 1879, p. 268, Legislative Manual for the State of Texas, 1879-1880, p. 268; 1882-3, pp. 264-265.

343 Anne Henderson Upton's tombstone in the Schulenberg Cemetery; Photographed by the Herzik Studio, May 7, 1957.

344 *Legislature Journal,* Regular Session, January 18, 1887, p. 289.

345 *Legislature Journal,* Regular Session, February 9, 1887, p. 301.

346 A certified death certificate from the Texas Department of Health, Bureau of Vital Statistics, to N. E. E., September 8, 1967.

347 *San Angelo Standard Times,* June 15, 1963.

348 *Ibid.,* September 25, 1966.　　349 *Ibid.,* June 15, 1963.

350 "Yates Revisited," *Marathon World,* Winter 1966, Vol. 3, No. 1, p. 19.

351 "First Oil West of the Pecos, Yates Field Hits the 40th Year," *Dallas Morning News,* October 30, 1966.

352 *Marathon World,* Winter 1966, Vol. 3, No. 1, p. 19.

353 *San Angelo Standard Times,* September 25, 1966.

354 *Ibid.*

355 Gene Keeney, Robt. Massie Funeral Chapel, to N. E. E., September 18, 1967.

APPENDIX I

COUNTY OFFICIALS

YEARS SERVED   OFFICE

From	To			Office
				County Judge
5-19-1910	11-13-1916	. . . .	L. W. Ainsworth
11-13-1916	8-25-1920	. . . .	H. B. Griffith
8-25-1920	12- 4-1920	. . . .	A. F. Schnaubert
12- 4-1920	1- 9-1922	. . . .	J. H. Felps
1- 9-1922	12-31-1928	. . . .	J. D. Patterson
1- 1-1929	12-31-1930	. . . .	C. H. Latson
1- 1-1931	12-31-1934	. . . .	M. L. Harris
1- 1-1935	12-31-1936	. . . .	M. T. Griffin
1- 1-1937	10-16-1942	. . . .	Ernest B. Van Zandt
11- 3-1942	12-31-1942	. . . .	C. G. Taylor
1- 1-1943	12-31-1946	. . . .	Wm. R. Edwards
1- 1-1947	12-31-1962	. . . .	G. H. Fisher
1- 1-1963		. . . .	Allen Moore

From	To			Office
				Commissioner, Precinct No. 1
5-19-1910	12-31-1910	. . . .	W. C. Summer
1- 1-1911	8-12-1912	. . . .	W. H. Underwood
8-12-1912	12-31-1914	. . . .	R. R. Bishop
1- 1-1915	11-13-1916	. . . .	Geo. E. Blanton
11-13-1916	8-24-1918	. . . .	D. M. Taylor
10-14-1918	9- 9-1922	. . . .	T. F. Hickox
9- 9-1922	5-11-1925	. . . .	R. W. Cushman
5-11-1925	1- 3-1926	. . . .	Jno. R. Johnston
1- 3-1927	12-31-1930	. . . .	J. W. Garner
1- 1-1931	12-31-1932	. . . .	J. D. Elder
1- 1-1933	2- 1-1939	. . . .	C. G. Taylor
2-13-1939	12-31-1942	. . . .	H. Wheeler
1- 1-1943	12-31-1944	. . . .	H. G. Yocham
1- 1-1945	12-31-1946	. . . .	Clint Shaw
1- 1-1947	12-31-1948	. . . .	H. G. Yocham
1- 1-1949	12-31-1956	. . . .	Sam Holmes
1- 1-1957		. . . .	H. Wheeler

From	To			Office
				Commissioner, Precinct No. 2
5-19-1910	4-17-1911	. . . .	J. W. Garner
5- 8-1911	11-13-1911	. . . .	J. A. Morrow
11-13-1911	11-12-1914	. . . .	J. G. Hall
12-14-1914	3- 8-1915	. . . .	Matt E. Mosely
4-19-1915	12-31-1915	. . . .	J. H. Fine
12-13-1915	11-14-1916	. . . .	J. G. Hall
5-14-1917	2-13-1918	. . . .	Tom Richardson
4- 8-1918	8-14-1920	. . . .	J. G. Hall

YEARS SERVED   OFFICE

From	*To*	*Commissioner, Precinct No. 2*
8-14-1920	9-20-1922	P. I. Elder
9-20-1922	11-21-1922	W. L. Gotcher
1- 1-1923	1- 3-1927	J. H. Massingill
1- 3-1927	12-31-1934	J. P. Rankin
1- 1-1935	12-31-1944	W. E. Yates
1- 1-1945	12-31-1952	W. J. Price
1- 1-1953		T. D. Workman, Jr.

From	*To*	*Commissioner, Precinct No. 3*
5-19-1910	5-18-1911	Jeff P. Thomason
1- 8-1912	12-31-1912	J. M. Sweatt
1- 1-1913	11-15-1913	C. T. Groves
2-11-1914	11-12-1914	J. H. Montgomery
1- 1-1915	8- 9-1915	C. A. Robinson
8- 9-1915	11-13-1916	J. H. Massingill
11-13-1916	8-17-1918	O. D. Windham
8-17-1918	12-31-1934	R. S. Windham
1- 1-1935	12-31-1938	Louis J. Feeler
1- 1-1939	12-31-1940	C. G. Harrall
1- 1-1941	12-31-1946	J. O. Currie
1- 1-1947	11- 2-1953	Tom Trimble
11- 2-1953	12-31-1954	W. W. Grief
1- 1-1955	12-31-1968	E. K. Buford
1- 1-1969		Kenneth D. LaQuey

From	*To*	*Commissioner, Precinct No. 4*
5-19-1910	12-12-1916	John F. Lane
12-12-1916	5-13-1918	I. S. Stovall
5-13-1918	8-24-1918	W. C. Lauman
3-10-1919	8-14-1920	G. W. Damron
8-14-1920	12- 4-1920	R. D. McSpadden
12- 4-1920	11- 4-1922	J. T. Holmes
11-21-1922	8-11-1924	Jno. R. Johnston
8-11-1924	12-31-1926	Cody Bell
1- 3-1927	8-20-1928	A. A. Bryant
8-20-1928	4-14-1930	V. D. Allen
4-14-1930	12-31-1934	James S. Key
1- 1-1935	12-31-1942	J. O. Carll
1- 1-1943	12-31-1946	Burley McCollum
1- 1-1947	12-31-1970	Joe E. Conger
1- 1-1971		Charles T. Fletcher

From	*To*	*Sheriff & Tax Collector*
5-19-1910	12-31-1914	A. F. Schnaubert
1- 1-1915	10-13-1917	J. D. Shoemake
10-13-1917	12-31-1922	J. W. Garner
1- 1-1923	6-25-1926	R. N. Stephenson
6-25-1926	12-31-1930	J. O. "Bud" Barfield
1- 1-1931	12-31-1934	W. C. Fowler

YEARS SERVED   OFFICE

From	To		Sheriff & Tax Assessor-Collector
1- 1-1935	12-31-1938	. . . .	W. C. Fowler
1- 1-1939	8-31-1945	. . . .	J. E. Simco
8-31-1945	12-31-1946	. . . .	Geo. Maley
1- 1-1947		. . . .	H. E. Eckols

From	To		Tax Assessor
5-19-1910	12-31-1912	. . . .	P. P. Barber
1- 1-1913	12-10-1917	. . . .	J. H. Johnson
12-10-1917	2-10-1919	. . . .	N. A. Zinn
2-10-1919	2-15-1921	. . . .	Dr. Homer Powers
2-15-1921	12-31-1928	. . . .	Mrs. N. O. Powers
1- 1-1929	12-31-1934	. . . .	R. N. Stephenson

From	To		County & District Clerk
5-19-1910	12- 4-1920	. . . .	R. C. Harlan
12- 4-1920	12-31-1930	. . . .	Maggie Taylor
1- 1-1931	12-31-1932	. . . .	J. C. Jackson
1- 1-1933	5-14-1952	. . . .	Ralph H. Daugherty
5-14-1952	12-31-1970	. . . .	Nancy Karen Daugherty
1- 1-1971		. . . .	Buena R. Coffee

From	To		County Treasurer
5-19-1910	5- 8-1911	. . . .	R. M. Johnson
5-13-1911	2-14-1912	. . . .	J. S. Stephenson
2-14-1912	8-27-1912	. . . .	D. B. Wyatt
8-27-1912	5-17-1913	. . . .	W. H. Kelly
5-17-1913	11-11-1914	. . . .	N. A. Zinn
11-11-1914	8-23-1919	. . . .	J. D. Patterson
8-23-1919	12- 4-1920	. . . .	Delia Lane
12- 4-1920	11- 3-1922	. . . .	Mrs. T. J. Holland
11- 3-1922	8-13-1923	. . . .	Mrs. O. B. Orr
8-13-1923	12-31-1926	. . . .	R. L. Harmon
1- 3-1927	12-31-1930	. . . .	L. L. Tierce
1- 1-1931	12-31-1934	. . . .	H. E. Hays
1- 1-1935	12-31-1938	. . . .	J. G. Long
1- 1-1939	12-31-1970	. . . .	Elizabeth L. Rains
1- 1-1971		. . . .	Doris L. Speed

From	To		County Attorney
5-19-1910	12-31-1912	. . . .	H. E. Webb
11-13-1916	12-31-1918	. . . .	W. D. Riser
11-10-1924	12-31-1926	. . . .	J. G. Smith
2-22-1926	1- 1-1927	. . . .	C. D. Spann
1- 3-1927	4-11-1927	. . . .	W. M. Davis
8-12-1927	12-31-1928	. . . .	W. M. Davis
1-10-1927	12-31-1927	. . . .	C. D. Spann (Civil Cases)
1- 1-1929	12-31-1940	. . . .	Hubert A. Foreman
1- 1-1941	12-31-1954	. . . .	John A. Menefee
1- 1-1955	12-31-1960	. . . .	Steve Preslar
1- 1-1961		. . . .	John A. Menefee

APPENDIX II

MONUMENT AT
McCAMEY DISCOVERY WELL

69.9 Feet North of this Marker

Spudded by McCamey & Brown, August 16, 1925

Brought in October 3, 1925

Monument erected by BOY SCOUTS Troop 31

McCamey, Texas, Unveiled February 15, 1931

TROOP ROSTER

J. M. Greenwood	*Scoutmaster*
Jas. W. Crowley	*Cons't. Supt. — Asst. S.M.*
Ray Clark	*Jr. Asst. S.M.*
Lloyd Byrd	*Jr. Asst. S.M.*
Leon Frieden	*Troop Scribe*
George Yamini	*Sr. P. L.*

John Berry	Darden McCollum	Woodrow Yamini, P. L.
Dick Lee	Charles David	Edwin Stafford
James Phinney	Tommy Service	James Hicks, P. L.
George Thaxton	Dean Carwile	Edgar Lee Pewitt
L. K. Trogden	Lee Burnham	Roy Mitchell
Joe Hudson	Jimmy Webb	Haywood Sturdivant
Thomas Lamb, P. L.	W. H. Gayle	Bill Meagher
Fred Senter	Malcolm Meyers	Weldon Gilliland
Marshall Middleton	Charles Vail	Dick Garrison, P. L.

TROOP SPONSORED BY McCAMEY LIONS CLUB

Appendix III

ADDRESS DELIVERED BY JUDGE PERRY PICKETT, MAY 28, 1960, AT THE OLD COURTHOUSE AT UPLAND, UPTON COUNTY, TEXAS

We have assembled here on this occasion to commemorate the Fiftieth Anniversary of the organization of Upton County.

My remarks shall be brief as befitting this occasion.

Let us turn the calendar back fifty years and try to picture this area as it was then.

William Howard Taft was President of the United States.

Thomas Mitchell Campbell was Governor of this great State of Texas.

Midland was then a small town with a population of 2,192.

It was four years before the outbreak of World War I. The nation was in a process of expansion. The western movement that had begun in the 1850's was reaching its climax. This area was still sparsely settled, some of it open country. The great migration and treks westward had been going on for some fifty to sixty years. Some came west for the excitement, some for the opportunity, the good along with the bad. We were still in the horse and buggy era although automobiles were coming into prominence. Seven years before the organization of this county, the Wright Brothers flew the first airplane. Some thirty years before the organization of this county, the iron horse had pushed across West Texas, the cross rails running some thirty-five miles to the north of us, west to El Paso, and the coast. Some of the range country had already begun to be fenced in, stock tanks were being built, and ranchers were consolidating their holdings. Game was still plentiful. An early settler would think nothing of riding his horse thirty to forty miles to a barbeque or dance.

Those early settlers and pioneers came into this country not as speculators bent on a quick profit and a hasty exit. They came seeking merely an opportunity — an opportunity to sink their roots, to wrest from the range a livelihood — knowing of the adversities they would face: the drought, sparse water, sandstorms, lean times, hard work, expecting little returns — the opportunity to make it on their own, to seek no quarter other than a chance. They were sturdy stock that came in wagons and buckboards with their earthly possessions aboard. The strong and the determined, the resourceful, the hard workers, the ones that never looked back, the ones that persevered and hung on, survived. The weak never made it.

They were an independent people, proud and with the indomitable spirit that made the West. Mind you, there were no oil and gas wells then, no paved roads, no fine schools, only open, raw range land. Through a cooperative spirit they started their schools and churches. They organized this county, they built this courthouse; we have here today descendants of those sturdy pioneers.

I have often heard it said by old timers that a man's word was his bond. A rancher's latchstring was always open to those who might stop by. They pitched in to help those who needed help.

Five decades later we have Upton County with a population of more than 8,000. You have fine schools, churches, recreational facilities, a healthy, vigorous poulation, with banks and business houses, a growing society.

It has taken all types of people to make this progress possible: the pioneer, the rancher, the oil companies, the business man, the whole strata of society.

To me, this old courthouse, now in ruins, serves as a fitting memorial in its bleak solitude, to those early settlers and pioneers, as a reminder of their sacrifices and their determination.

I shall relate a few facts about Upton County:

Upton County was created out of Tom Green County, February 26, 1887. The county was named for Colonel John Upton who was killed in the 2nd Battle of Manassas, and for his brother, the Honorable William F. Upton.

For judicial purposes Upton was joined to Midland County for a number of years.

The State Legislature was petitioned for county organization in 1910, with Upland as the county seat. Petition was granted and the following officers elected:

L. W. Ainsworth . . . . County Judge

A. F. Schnaubert . . . . Sheriff

R. C. Harlan . . . . County & Dist. Clerk

W. C. Summer, J. W. Garner,
Jeff P. Thomason, and John F. Lane . . . . Commissioners

In 1900 only 48 people lived in the county.

The real estate of M. Halff & Son owned a section of land near the old stage stand on which they mapped out the townsite, Upland, including a Courthouse square.

On January 17, 1914, the Upland Courthouse was approved by the Commissioners' Court. It was built by a Dallas firm at a cost of $22,000.00. Another building was used for a courthouse prior to this time.

In 1911 about 200 people lived in Upland.

In 1908 Midland County granted a petition for a school at Upland.

When the Orient Railroad came through the county about 1911 or 1912, people left Upland and moved to Rankin.

The town of Rankin was named for F. E. Rankin, who donated half a section of land for the townsite.

By 1918 few people were left in Upland.

In 1925 when the first oil well blew in, the town of Crossett and McCamey sprang up. McCamey finally swallowed the town of Crossett.

The estimated county population in 1957 was just under 8,000.

In closing, I would like to say that it took a lot of shoulders to the wheel to get Upton County to 1960. Can we not say that in 2010, at your Centennial, that you people of 1960 carried on in the tradition of those of 1910?

Speaking for all West Texans, I congratulate you and commend you on this, your Fiftieth Anniversary.

APPENDIX IV

UPTON COUNTY NEWSPAPERS

Upland Roundup: September 16, 1910-1915. W. D. Riser, Publisher.

Rankin News: 1915-1926. W. D. Riser, Publisher.

Rankin Register: 1927. ("a flash in the pan") Lasted less than a year. B. B. Yantis, Publisher.

Upton County Journal: November 17, 1927. B. W. Barnes, Publisher. In less than a year his son-in-law, C. L. Burress, succeeded him as publisher and continued the ownership until 1945.

Rankin News: Was published in McCamey from 1945 to 1952. Jim Carll purchased the Upton County Journal from Mrs. C. L. Burress in 1945 and was sole owner until April 6, 1946, when he and his brother, C. C. Carll, became equal partners. They changed the name to Rankin News, and C. C. Carll became the sole owner and publisher April 17, 1947. He continued publishing the paper in McCamey until 1952, at which time he re-equipped the Rankin plant.

Rankin News: In 1953 J. B. Hutchens, Jr. of Slaton, Texas, took over as publisher and now has complete ownership of the paper.[1]

Mrs. Ann Clark to N. E. E.; and Bob Horn, *Odessa American*, July 30, 1967.

McCamey Tri-County Record: September 16, 1926 — September 1929, W. D. Riser, Publisher. (Riser picked that name because he intended to serve McCamey, Crane and Iraan, all in three separate counties)

McCamey Daily Telegram: Published every Tuesday while the Tri-County Record was published on Friday. (W. D. Riser, Publisher)[2]

McCamey Leader: 1929. R. A. Hall, Publisher.

McCamey News: September, 1929 — March, 1932. A. Garland Adair, Publisher, who bought and consolidated the McCamey Tri-County Record, the McCamey Daily Telegram and the McCamey Leader.[3]

McCamey News: Spring, 1932. Martin Publishing Company. J. L. Martin, Sr., Publisher, and son, Jimmy Martin, Editor, took over the operation until June 2, 1943, when they sold it to Mrs. C. L. Burress, who was the publisher of the Upton County Journal in Rankin. (Her husband had gone into military service.[4]) Mrs. Burress leased the McCamey News to Jim Carll, and the two jointly published the McCamey and the Rankin Weeklies in Rankin.

McCamey News: December, 1944. Mrs. Burress and Jim Carll were co-publishers in McCamey until March, 1945, when Carll became the sole owner until April 6, 1946.

McCamey News: April 6, 1946 — April 17, 1947, C. C. Carll and his brother, Jim Carll, were equal partners as publishers.

McCamey News: April 17, 1947, to the present C. C. Carll is the full owner and publisher of the McCamey News.

[1] Anniversary Edition of the *Rankin News*, May 26, 1960. Vol. XXXV No. 31; and
[2] *McCamey News*, June 23, 1960.
[3] Bob Horn, *Odessa American*, August 8, 1967.
[4] Letter from Mrs. C. L. Burress to Mrs. Ann Clark, 1968.

APPENDIX V

McELROY RANCH COMPANY

1. November 1, 1906, John S. Ely of Linn County, Iowa, sold to John T. McElroy of Midland County, Texas, 54 sections (34,560 acres) by warranty deed for $41,040.00. Upton County Deed Records, Vol. 2, page 287.

2. John T. McElroy, February 8, 1926, leased for oil and gas to William H. Dunning, Jr., Upton County Deed Records, Vol. 17, page 212.

3. William H. Dunning, Jr., November 3, 1926, leased for oil and gas to the Gulf Production Company, Vol. 24, page 500.

4. John T. McElroy on March 3, 1927, sold to Henry A. deCompiegne of Denver, Colorado, the minerals and 68,720 acres and over 6,000 cattle and all horses and mules for $2,500,000.00. Vol. 26, page 420.

5. Henry A. deCompiegne sold to McElroy Ranch Company, March 23, 1927, 69,360 acres with personal property and minerals. Vol. 28, page 104.

6. McElroy Ranch Company sold to Franco-Western Oil Company by resolution July 7, 1961. Vol. 305, page 43.

7. Franco-Western Oil Company merged with parent company, Franco-Wyoming Oil Company, September 28, 1964. Vol. 351, page 39.

8. Franco-Wyoming Oil Company sold oil interests to Warren and Company, September 1, 1965, for $30,000,000.00 for minerals only. Vol. 357, page 115.

9. Franco-Wyoming Oil Company by warranty deed sold to Clinton Manges Trustee surface ranch house and stock on October 29, 1965. Vol. 362, page 144.

Upton County Archives, Edith Windham, Archivist.

APPENDIX VI

TEXAS STATE HISTORICAL SURVEY COMMITTEE OF UPTON COUNTY

1971

Committee Chairman . . . . Mrs. Billie Sue Doucette

Vice-Chairman . . . . Mrs. Edith Windham

Secretary & Treasurer . . . . Mrs. Jack Smith

Reporter . . . . Mrs. Ann Clark

Sub-Committee Chairmen are:

Historical Preservation Committee . . . . Mrs. Billie Sue Doucette,
Mrs. Edith Windham and N. Ethie Eagleton

Historical Marker Committee . . Mr. George Ramer and Miss Maggie Taylor

History Appreciation Committee . . . . Mrs. Ann Clark, Mrs. Peggy Garner
and Mrs. Gerry Waddell

Advisory Committee . . . . Mrs. Opal Nix, Mrs. Jack Smith
and Mrs. Anna Wolf

Finance and Budget Committee . . . County Judge Allen Moore (Chairman)
H. Wheeler, T. D. Workman, Jr., Kenneth D. LaQuey and
Charles T. Fletcher, County Commissioners
Mayor A. B. Epley and Mayor J. P. Pettit
Johnnie Hurst

APPENDIX VII

UPTON COUNTY HISTORICAL MARKERS

Adrian House[2] (1964)
Benedum Oil Field & Townsite[3] (1963)
Bobcat Hills[3] (1965)
Burton-Lingo[2] (1964)
Castle Gap (Site)[2] (1962)
Castle Gap (Highway)[4] (1963)
Castle Mountain[3] (1967)
Castle Mountain Park[3] (1968)
Elliott Ranch House[2] (1964)
First Humble Oil Camp[3] (1967)
King Mountain[3] (1968)
Little House On The Corner[4] (1967)
McCamey Junior High School[3] (1968)
McCamey Marker[3] (1964)
Mendoza Trail Museum[3] (1967)
Radford Grocery[2] (1964)

Rankin[3] (1964)
Rattlesnake Butte[3] (1967)
Square Top Mountain[3] (1968)
Table Top Mountain[3] (1968)
Upland Courthouse[2] (1960)
Upland County Seat[2] (1964)
Upton County (Centennial)[1] (1936)
Upton, Jno. C. and Wm. F.[5] (1964)
Weir No. 1[3] (1964)
Yates Hotel[2] (1964)

---

[1] *Centennial Markers*
[2] *Upton County Historical Society*
[3] *Upton County Historical Survey
Committee*
[4] *C. W. Brown*
[5] *State Matching Fund*

BIBLIOGRAPHY

LETTERS:

Berry, Mrs. Marie, San Antonio Public Library, to N. E. E., March 16, 1965.

Chadwell, Patricia, Fort Worth Public Library, to N. E. E., October 22, 1965.

Day, Dr. James M., Texas State Archives, Austin, Texas, to N. E. E., March 5, 1965.

Freeman, Ernestine Halff (Mrs. Norman), Dallas, Texas, to N. E. E., September 9, 1963; May 9, 1964; October 22, 1964; December 15, 1964; February 1, 1965; September 9, 1965; September 28, 1965; October 18, 1965; January 25, 1966.

Freytag, Walter F., La Grange, Texas, to N. E. E., April 18, 1957.

Halff, M. H. to Misses Maggie Taylor and N. E. E., July 27, 1964; and to N. E. E., October 14, 1964; October 22, 1964.

Hart, Henry M., Vice Chairman Executive Committee, Bank of Commerce, San Antonio, Texas, to Derwood Langston, President Security State Bank, McCamey, Texas, April 2, 1965.

Hopson, Edith, Trans Pecos Abstract Co., Alpine, Texas, to N. E. E., January 21, 1966.

Keeney, Gene, Robt. Massie Funeral Chapel, San Angelo, Texas, to N. E. E., September 18, 1967.

Langdon, Jim C., Austin, Texas, to N. E. E., October 6, 1964.

Lowery, Dunn, President First State Bank of Rankin, Texas, to George W. Ramer, President Upton County Historical Society, October 25, 1968.

Navarro, Sue (Mrs. M. E.,), President Reeves County Historical Survey Committee, to N. E. E., November 29, 1965; December 12, 1965.

Perry, Mrs. Carmen, D. R. T. Library at the Alamo, to N. E. E., December 21, 1964.

Phillips, Mrs. Ada, Midland, Texas, to N. E. E., October 11, 1965.

Pickett, Ellen, Liberty, Texas, to N. E. E., December 1, 1964; January 27, 1965; December 28, 1965.

Powell, Leta, Ozona, County Clerk, Crockett County, Texas, to N. E. E., March 27, 1965.

Sadler, Jerry, Austin, Texas, to N. E. E., February 19, 1965; April 26, 1966.

Santos, Richard, Bexar County Archivist, San Antonio, Texas, to N. E. E., December 16, 1964; July 20, 1965.

Simpson, Col. H. B., Hillsboro, Texas, to N. E. E., May 16, 1963.

Wedin, Mrs. Frank, Marathon, Texas, to N. E. E., November 20, 1965.

INTERVIEWS:

Barfield, E. E. to N. E. E., September 15, 1966.

Cole, John to N. E. E., October 12, 1968.

Earnest, Mrs. Effie to N. E. E., July 12, 1963.

Gibson, Judge Aileen to N. E. E., July 27, 1953.

Hinde, Mrs. Hattie to N. E. E., April 20, 1944. (Confirmed by her daughter, Crescendze Hinde, October 12, 1968.)

Inghram, B. B., Ozona, Texas, to N. E. E., July 10, 1960.

Nix, Mrs. Opal, Rankin, Texas, to N. E. E., June 16, 1967.

Price, Dave, McCamey, Texas, to N. E. E., September 16, 1963.

Price, Mrs. Dave, McCamey, Texas, to N. E. E., September 16, 1963.

Ramer, George, McCamey, Texas, to N. E. E., October 12, 1968.

Scott, Allie V., McCamey, Texas, to N. E. E., April 20, 1965.

NEWSPAPERS:

Big Lake Wildcat, May 5, 1966.

Dallas Herald, February 24, 1881; March 10, 1881; March 17, 1881; February 9, 1882; January 11, 1883; December 25, 1884; August 28, 1884.

Dallas Morning News, October 30, 1966.

Fort Worth Star-Telegram, June 1, 1958.

Houston Daily Post, February 20, 23, 1881; March 1, 3, 8, 16, 17, 27, 29, 30, 31, 1881; February 23, 1882; March 1, 4, 9, 15, 1882; March 13, 1883; January 13, 1884; February 9, 1884; June 4, 8, 1884.

McCamey News, May 13, 1938; August 18, 1950; June 23, 1955; January 12, 1956; June 23, 1960; December 20, 1962; January 2, 1965; June 24, 1965; October 27, 1966.

Midland Reporter-Telegram, October 18, 1953.

San Angelo Standard Times, August 25, 1950; June 15, 1963; October 18, 1964; November 17, 1964; March 25, 1965; October 28, 1965; February 12, 1966; June 19, 1966; September 25, 1966; November 10, 1966; February 3, 1967; May 28, 1967.

Pecos Enterprise, October 16, 1936, Microfilm from Reeves County Library; and Fiftieth Anniversary Edition. (No date) Follows July 31, 1935.

MANUSCRIPTS:

Bone, Margaret (Mrs. E. C.). A brief biography of her mother, Mrs. Margaret Littlejohn, October 25, 1968.

Dusterwick, Fred. "A History of the McElroy Ranch," Unpublished, 1950.

Halff, M. H. "A Brief Biography of Henry M. Halff," Unpublished, 1964.

Howard, Mabel (Mrs. Harry). "A Brief Biography of Mr. and Mrs. John F. Lane," Unpublished, 1967.

Howard, Scotty. "John F. Lane," Unpublished, 1950.

Johnson, Alma Mae (Mrs. Theodore Willis). "A Brief Biography of Theodore Willis Johnson," Unpublished, 1967.

McCamey, Olive (Mrs. George B.). "A Short Biography of George B. McCamey," January 30, 1968.

McKinley, Nancy Rankin (Mrs.). "Biographical Sketch of Finis Ewing and Eliza Rankin," Unpublished, 1967.

Nix, Mrs. Opal. "Mountains and Buttes in Southwestern Upton County," Unpublished, 1965.

Patterson, Paul. "Memoirs of His Father, Judge Patterson," Unpublished, June 14, 1967.

Ramer, George. "Mrs. Walter Harris," Unpublished, 1960.

Russell, Lelyle (Harris). "The Kansas City, Mexico, and Orient Railway Company of Texas," Unpublished, 1946.

Smith, Don C. "Smith's Folly," Unpublished, December 20, 1955.

Van Atta, W. L. "Wild Life in Upton County," Upton County Historical Society, 1956.

PAMPHLETS, BULLETINS AND RECORDS:

Allcorn, Bill. *History of Texas Land.* Austin, 1958.

Conner, H. B. "Valuable Plants Native to Texas," *Bulletin of Texas Agricultural and Mechanical College.* College Station, August, 1937.

Cory, V. L. and H. B. Parks. "Catalogue of the Flora of the State of Texas," *Bulletin of the Texas Agricultural College.* College Station, July, 1937.

Eagleton, N. Ethie. "An Historic Indian Cache in Pecos County," *Bulletin of the Texas Archaeological Society,* Vol. 26, (October, 1955).

Giles, Bascom. *History and Disposition of Texas Public Domain.* Austin, 1945.

Hutchison, J. E. *Know Your Grasses.* College Station, no date.

Lang, A. S. *Financial History of the Public Lands of Texas.* Waco, 1932.

Native Flora of Texas. Austin, no date.

"Soil Survey (Reconnaisance of West-Central Texas 1922)," United States Department of Agriculture, Washington, 1928.

Williams, O. W. *Historic Review Animal Life in Pecos County.* Dallas, 1908.

"A Certified Birth Certificate of Arthur Caldwell II," Texas Department of Health, Bureau of Vital Statistics, Austin.

"A Certified Death Certificate of Ira G. Yates," Texas Department of Health, Bureau of Vital Statistics, Austin.

DEED RECORDS, MINUTES AND JOURNALS:

Brewster (Buchel) County Deed Records — Vol. I: 164; 216.

Crockett County Deed Records — Vol. I: 391; II: 95-98; III: 174; IV: 276; 348; 350; VI: 450; VII: 370; 375; 416; VIII: 81; 110; 343; 508; 509; IX: 188; X: 264; 361.

Midland County Commissioners' Court Minutes — Vol. II: 527-528.

Pecos County Deed Records — Vol. XCV: 195.

Upton County Deed Records — Vol I: 20-21; 88-92; 130-140; 313; 380; II: 20-21; 161-163; 287; 311; 313; 387; IV: 264; X: 495-538; XII: 223; XXVI: 27; 46; 61; 82; 339; 563.

Upton County Commissioners' Court Minutes — Vol. I: 64; 70; 98; 102; 146; IV: 107.

Journal of the House of Representatives of the Regular Sessions of: The Eleventh Session of the State of Texas, Austin; the Sixteenth Session of the State of Texas, Austin; the Seventeenth Session of the State of Texas, Austin; the Eighteenth Session of the State of Texas, Austin; the Nineteenth Session of the State of Texas, Austin, and the Called Session of the Seventeenth Legislature, Austin, 1889. (1876-1889).

Legislative Manual for the State of Texas: 1879-1880; 1882-1883 (Austin, E. W. Swindells).

Legislature Journal, Regular Session, February 9, 1887.

Minutes of the McCamey Independent District School Board — April 21, 1941; 1942; April 9, 1947; July 5, 1949; October 12, 1949; November 9, 1949; January 11, 1950. (No page numbers).

Minutes of the McCamey Women's Study Club — 1929; 1929-1930; 1942-1943; 1943-1944; 1944-1945.

THESES AND FOUNDATIONS:

Dod, Catherine. *A History of Education in Upton County*, M.A. Thesis, Sul Ross State College, Alpine, Texas.

McQuary, Rena. *A Survey of Education in Upton County 1904-1944*, M.A. Thesis, Hardin-Simmons University, Abilene, 1945.

Benedum, Paul G. *Claude Worthington Benedum Foundation Cumulative Report 1944-1962*. (Benedum Trees Building, Pittsburg, Pennsylvania).

BOOKS:

Cooke, Philip St. George, William H. Whiting and F. X. Aubry, *Exploring Southwestern Trails*. Glendale: Arthur H. Clark Co., 1938.

Conkling, Roscoe and Margaret Conkling. *The Butterfield Overland Mail, 1857-1869*, Glendale: Arthur H. Clark Co., 1947.

Cox, James. *Historical and Biographical Record of the Cattle Industry and the Cattlemen of Texas and the Adjacent Territory*. St. Louis, 1895.

Daniell, Ellis A. and Edwin H. Grobe (eds.). *New Encyclopedia of Texas*. Dallas: Texas Development Bureau.

Davis, Ellis Arthur (ed.). *The Historical Encyclopedia of Texas*, Dallas: Texas Development Bureau.

Fulmore, Z. T. *The History and Geography of Texas As Told In County Names*. Austin: The Steck Co., 1935.

Gammel, H. P. N. (ed.) *The Laws of Texas, 1822-1897*. Austin: Gammell Book Co. 1898.

Giles, Bascom and Curtis Bishop. *Lots of Land*. Austin: The Steck Co., 1949.

Henderson, Harry McCorry. *Texas in the Confederacy*. San Antonio: The Naylor Co., 1955.

Hunter J. Marvin. *The Trail Drivers of Texas*. Nashville: Cokesburg Press, 1925.

Jones, Billy M. *The Search for Maturity 1875-1900*. Austin: Steck-Vaughn Co. 1965.

Larson, Henrietta M. and Kenneth Wiggin Porter. *History of Humble Oil and Refining Company*. New York: Harper and Brothers, 1959.

Loughery, E. H. *Personnel of the Texas State Government*. Austin: L. E. Daniell, 1885.

Mallison, Sam. *The Great Wildcatter, The Story of Mike Benedum*. Charleston: Education Foundation of West Virginia, Inc. 1953.

McCoy, Joseph G. *Historic Sketches of the Cattle Trade of the West and Southwest*. Glendale: Arthur H. Clark and Company, 1940.

McKay, Seth and Odie B. Faulk. *Texas After Spindletop*. Austin: Steck-Vaughn Company, 1965.

Marshall, James. *Santa Fe, the Railroad that Built an Empire*. New York: Random House, 1945.

Monuments Erected by the State of Texas to Commemorate the Centenary of Texas Independence. Austin: The Steck Company, 1939.

Nordyke, Lewis. *The Great Roundup: The Story of Texas and the Southwestern Cowmen*. New York: Morrow, 1955.

Ormsby, Waterman L. *The Butterfield Overland Mail*. Edited by W. L. Wright and T. Bynum. San Marino: The Huntington Library, 1954.

Paddock, Capt. B. B. *History and Biographical Record of North and West Texas.* Chicago: The Lewis Publishing Company, 1906.

Polley, J. B. *Hood's Texas Brigade, Its Marches, Battles and Achievements.* Neale Publishing Company, 1910.

Richardson, Rupert N. *The Comanche Barrier to the South Plains Settlement.* Glendale: A. H. Clark and Company, 1933.

Rister, Carl Coke. *The Southwestern Frontier, 1865-1881.* Glendale: The Arthur H. Clark Company, 1928.

Peyton, Green. *America's Heartland, The Southwest.* Norman: The University of Oklahoma Press, 1948.

Schwettman, Martin W. *Santa Rita.* Austin: The Texas Historical Association, 1943.

Tharp, Benjamin Carrol. *Texas Range Grasses.* Austin: The University Press, 1952.

Wallace, Ernest. *Texas In Turmoil.* Austin: Steck-Vaughn Company, 1965.

Webb, Walter Prescott. *The Great Plains.* Dallas: Ginn and Company, 1931.

Webb, Walter Prescott et al. *The Handbook of Texas.* Austin: The Texas State Historical Association, 1952.

MAGAZINES:

Baggett, W. R. "Early Day Irrigation Ditches on the Pecos," *Frontier Times* XIX, 1942.

Baron, Ronald. "Canyon Creed," *Junior Historian* XIII, 1952.

Bender, A. B. "Opening Routes Across West Texas 1840-1850," *Southwestern Historical Quarterly.* XXXVII, 1933. and "The Texas Frontier, 1848-1861," XXXVIII, 1934.

Biesele, R. L. "The German Settlers and The Indians in Texas," *Southwestern Historical Quarterly.* XXXI, 1927.

Bingham, Betty Marie. "Major Ben Ficklin," *Junior Historian,* XXI, 1960.

Broussard, John. "Arthur Stilwell's Dream City," *Junior Historian,* XXI, 1960.

Brown, Josie (Schnaubert). "Arthur Francis Schnaubert," *Junior Historian,* IX, 1949.

Caldwell, Arthur III. "Mike Benedum and the Permian Basin," *Junior Historian,* XVII, 1956; and, "Upton County's Uptons," XIX, 1958.

Carnahan, Arthur L. "Texas Collection," *Southwestern Historical Quarterly.* Vol. 53, 1950; Vol. 54, 1951.

Dobie, J. Frank. "The First Cattle in Texas and the Progenitors of the Longhorns," *Southwestern Historical Quarterly,* XLII, 1939.

Eagleton, N. Ethie. "Dunes, Deserts and Mesas, Their Early Indian Life," *The Naturalist,* XII, Summer, 1961.

Garner, Peggy Sue (Mrs. Jack). "Early Days in Upton County," *Junior Historian,* VIII, 1948.

Hamilton, Elizabeth (Cope). "McCamey's Water Supply," *Junior Historian,* V, 1944.

Holmes, Tomie. "Thomas Stonehouse," *Junior Historian,* XII, 1952.

Humble Oil and Refining Company. *Humble Way.* Houston: Humble Oil and Refining Company.

Jones, Don. "Dr. Homer Powers, A Pioneer Physician," *Junior Historian,* XIV, 1954.

The Liner, V. Humble Pipe Line Company, May, 1966.

Locklin, Billy. "Coyotes and No Fences," *Junior Historian*, XV, 1955.

"Yates Revisited," *Marathon World*. Vol. 3, (Winter, 1966).

Martin, Jimmy. *West Texas Electric Times*, February, 1950; September, 1950.

Martin, Mabelle Eppard. "California Emigrant Roads Through Texas," *Southwestern Historical Quarterly*, XXVIII, 1925.

Neighbors, Kenneth F., "The Expedition of Major Robert S. Neighbors in 1849," *Southwestern Historical Quarterly*, LVIII, 1954.

Selby, Yvonne (Johnson). "The Old 'Dobe Crossing," *Junior Historian*, V, 1945.

Stewart, Loretta. "The Fisher-Miller Lands," *Junior Historian*, XI, 1950.

White, Grace Miller. "The Activities of M. Halff and Brother," *Frontier Times*, XIX, 1942.

TAPE RECORDINGS:

Dedication Ceremony, Upton, William Felton and Upton, John C. Rankin, Upton County Courthouse, Master of Ceremonies — County Judge Allen Moore, November 11, 1963.

Gill, Cecil, Display Department of Humble Oil Company; interview describes the Relief Map of Upton County, August 15, 1957.

Huffman, Leeland, Assistant Superintendent of Humble Pipe Line; Division Dedicatory Speech of Relief Map of Upton County, October 14, 1957.

Kelton, Buck, Manager McElroy Ranch, interviewed by LuAnn Kelton, August 23, 1964.

Littlejohn, Margaret; Bone, Margaret; Ramer, George W.; Wolf, William; Wolf, Mrs. William; Historical Review of Early Day Life in McCamey, April 15, 1957.

Locklin, Dee, "Santa Rita," interviewed by N. E. E., October 20, 1960.

McCamey, George B., "The Discovery Well," June 21, 1957.

Nevill, Mr. and Mrs. V. G., "Along the Pecos River, 1908-1963." Interviewed by N. E. E., September 15, 1963.

Newland, Cliff, Windmiller for the McElroy Ranch. Interviewed by Elmer Kelton, August 23, 1964.

Patterson, Paul, "Strange Changes on the Range," Interviewed by Elmer Kelton, W. W. A., President, Odessa, June 18, 1963.

Ramer, George W., "The McCamey Water Supply," June 21, 1957.

INDEX

122   *INDEX*

Pontotoc, Texas, 71
Pool, S. P., 23
Poole, Iona, 20, 21
Port Isabel, Texas, 58
Porter, Barbara Johnson, 87
Porter, Kenneth Wiggins, 91, 92, 110
Post Office Park, McCamey, 38
Potomac Defense Line, Virginia, 81
Potosie, Texas, 34
Powell Gap, 6
Powell, Leta, 107
Powell Oil Field, 30, 32, 73
Powers, Dr. Homer, 24, 73, 74, 100
Powers, Mr. & Mrs., 73
Powers, Mrs. N. O., 100
Prescott, Arizona, 64
Presidio County, Texas, 67
Preslar, Steve, 100
Prettyman, T. M., 22
Price, D. M., 16
Price, Dave, 13, 16, 17, 58, 88, 94, 108
Price, Mrs. Dave, 16, 88, 108
Price, Howard W., 32
Price, W. J., 99
Proctor, Leonard, 30
Purple Heart, 78

Quien Sabe Ranch & Stock, 10, 58, 60

Radford Grocery Marker, 106
Radford Grocery No. 1, 46
Railroad Lands, 12, 14
Rains, Mrs. Elizabeth L., 100
Ramer, George W., 28, 30, 32, 33, 44,
    90, 92, 94, 97, 106, 108, 112
Ramer, Mrs. George W., 42, 92
Rankin Cemetery, 55, 62
Rankin, City of, 4, 11, 14, 18, 19, 20, 21,
    22, 23, 24, 25, 38, 42, 44, 46, 56, 62,
    64, 66, 67, 72, 74, 75, 80, 83, 84, 103,
    104
        Rankin Marker, 106
        Post Office, 22
Rankin County Hospital District, 39
Rankin Creek, 2
Rankin, Eliza Smith, 74, 75
Rankin, Finis Ewing, 18, 74, 75, 79, 103
Rankin, Jesse Pearl, 25, 74, 99
Rankin, Maude, 74, 75
Rankin News, 104
Rankin, F. E. Ranch, 75
Rankin Register, 104
Rankin, Robert Donnell & Matilda
    Lynch, 74
Rankin, Robert Porter, 74
Rankin Independent School District, 23,
    25, 34, 63
        High School Band, 40
Rankin Women's Study Club, 37, 38, 62
Rappahannock Defense Line, Virginia,
    81
Rattlesnake Butte, 1, 4, 23
Rattlesnake Butte Marker, 106
Rattlesnake Derby, 31

Reagan County, Texas, 11, 12, 19, 42,
    46, 51, 63, 71
Rebecca Lodge, McCamey, Texas, 37
Reeves County, Texas, 69, 73
Reichelderfer, F. W., 86
Reimers, Mrs. F. C., 37
Republic Production Company, 35, 43
Resser, Charles E., 86
Richardson, Rupert N., 111
Richardson, S. O., 13, 14
Richardson, Texas, 59
Richardson, Tom, 98
Ridgeway, Pennsylvania, 65
Rio Grande River, 6, 20
Riser, W. D., 22, 27, 30, 100, 104
Rister, Carl Coke, 111
Robbins, J. W. "Jim," 19, 21, 42
Roberts, Frank H. H., 86
Robinson, C. A., 99
Robinson, J. T., 88
Rochester, New York, 79
Rodman, E. G., 46, 47
Rodman-Noel Oil Field, 46, 47
Round Rock, Texas, 62
Royal Countess, a horse, 68
Roznov, Texas, 57
Rudicille, Rankin, 34
Russel, H. H., 19
Russell, Lelyle Harris, 97, 108
Russell, W. E., 30

S Ranch, 76
Sabeata, 6
Sacred Heart Catholic Church,
    McCamey, 33
Sadler, Jerry, 107
Salado River, 6
Salt Creek, 76
Salt Crossing, 73
Saltenberg, August, 6
Salvation Annie Yates Memorial Citadel,
    85
San Angelo, Texas, 10, 12, 20, 21, 30, 32,
    45, 55, 62, 63, 73, 74, 78, 79, 80, 83,
    84, 85
San Angelo Standard Times, 108
San Antonio, Texas, 8, 9, 52, 55, 58, 60
San Francisco, California, 7
San Saba County, Texas, 63
Sangre de Cristo Mountains, 5
Santa Anita, California, 68
Santa Fe Park, 38, 39, 44
Santa Fe Railroad, 26, 32, 46
Santa Rita (Oil Field), 30
Santa Rita No. 1, 42, 45
Santos, Richard G., 93, 107
Satterwhite, C. M., 45
Sawtelle, Gilbert, 34
Schilling, E. A., 40
Schiwetz, Buck, 44
Schnaubert, Arthur Francis, 10, 11, 13,
    14, 16, 17, 19, 20, 21, 75, 76, 77, 98,
    99, 103
Schnaubert, Marie Null, 75

Designed by

E. HAYWOOD ANTONE